Endorseme
for <u>Deception</u>!

As Christians, we have a mighty Saviour. But we also have a powerful enemy, who ceaselessly attacks those who 'keep God's commands and hold fast their testimony about Jesus' (Revelation 12:17). The 'father of lies' (John 8:44) sets out to deceive individuals, even whole nations. This book gives a clear and engaging overview of what the Bible teaches about this cosmic conflict; warns about contemporary challenges to truth; and offers helpful guidance on how to proclaim biblical truth in our current cultural moment.

Dr Sharon James
The Christian Institute, UK

Satan is not someone we talk much about in the modern church and it shows. The father of lies is swindling our post-truth culture of anything good, true, and beautiful. This cannot be ignored. Lee Emerson's new book *Deception!* is a biblically insightful guide, helping us understand and resist Satan's deceit so that we might stand for truth. I highly recommend it!

Andy Steiger
President, Apologetics Canada

A sobering tour through the Bible and the culture, unmasking the way the Devil uses lies and deception to destroy humanity; it left me realising I'd been ill-informed and naïve about this central aspect of the Christian's spiritual battle. It was a real stimulus to prayer.

Rico Tice
All Souls Church & Christianity Explored

With a magisterial survey of scripture and wise application to life, this book reminds us that as we look back to the cross and await the return of Jesus, the Christian life is a battle, not against flesh and blood but against the principalities and powers in the heavenly realms. When our hearts and minds as so often dulled by the deceit which surrounds us, this is a book we need to read. It is both a much-needed wake-up call and food for the soul.

Simon Austen
Rector, St Leonards Church, Exeter

THE CRAFT OF SATAN, THE FOLLY OF MAN,
THE WISDOM OF GOD

DECEPTION!

LEE N. EMERSON

FOREWORD BY DAVID JACKMAN

Vide Press
6200 Second Street
Washington D.C. 20011
www.VidePress.com

ISBN: 978–1–954618–28–2 (Print)
ISBN: 978–1–954618–07–7 (eBook)

Printed in the United States of America

Cover designed by MiblArt.com

Table of Contents

Acknowledgements

I have been much helped and encouraged, and sometimes corrected, in the writing of this manuscript by the comments of friends and fellow-elders and -pastors, including Steve Owen, Oliver Ward, Rev. Mike Fox, and Dr. Mark Carpenter — all gave their time unselfishly to reading the draft and feeding back instructive comments. David Jackman kindly agreed not only to do these things, but also to add his own comments in the *Foreword*. I owe David a considerable debt of gratitude going back to my own early days as a Christian, when he helped me to discern true from false in much that presented itself as Christian wisdom and practice. I would like to thank Jeffry Parker at *Vide Press* who read the manuscript, quickly grasped its message, and has pushed it forward; he has made it very easy for me to navigate the path of a first-time author. I would also like to thank the congregation of Scott Drive Church here in Exmouth, Devon, for their support of me over many years, which has given me the opportunity to think about the subject of this book, and time to put pen to paper. Lastly, I would like to thank my wife (Annette), and children (Ruth and Thomas), for their contribution — as I am sure is the case for many other families, they have helped me to see things I would not have been able to see on my own, as well as showing me the necessary forbearance when I have retreated into the study.

Soli Deo Gloria

Foreword

This is a much-needed book. When the apostle Paul has concluded his magisterial survey of the gospel, in the first eleven chapters of his letter to the Christians in Rome, he immediately turns from his eulogy of "the depth of the riches of the wisdom and knowledge of God" to warning his readers of a present and serious danger. "Do not conform any longer to the pattern of this world, but be transformed by the renewing of your mind" (Rom 12:2). As one paraphrase expresses it, "Don't let the world squeeze you into its mould." That is a continuing challenge and concern for Christian believers in every era. We may know, trust, and rejoice in the great truths of the gospel, but be almost oblivious as to how the world is subtly squeezing us into its thought-forms and patterns of behavior. Like the proverbial frog in a pot, we may not perceive the danger as the temperature of the water is gradually increased, until it is too late to escape.

One of the most important duties of the faithful pastor-teacher is to relate the clear teaching of Scripture to the pressing and urgent issues of our own time. While the Bible's truth is eternal and unchanging, it has to be applied to a different set of historical circumstances, a different cultural milieu, in every generation, and if those connections are not being made the teaching will not be fully faithful to the inspired text. The purpose of God's revelation is not simply a formulation of the truth (which can become quite abstract) but a radical change of character and life-style in those who receive it.

We live in an extraordinary historical context where false ideas, distortions, and denials of truth abound and seem only to multiply exponentially with every new development of information technology. The whole world may never have been better connected, but it has also never had so much difficulty and confusion in seeking to answer the question, "What is truth?"

So, what are we Christians to do about it? It may be tempting to wring our hands in despair, bemoan the global problems, but effectively put up the shutters and decide that we prefer not to know. That is to be the frog in the boiling pot!

In this insightful and significant book, Lee Emerson, a wise and experienced pastor-teacher over many years, shows us a better and thoroughly Biblical course of action, as he speaks the unchanging truth of Scripture into the cultural dilemmas and confusing delusions of our day. This is a book to challenge and transform our thinking through the straightforward explanation and application of God's eternal truth to God's people, in a rapidly changing world. The narrative which flows through these chapters follows the trajectory of Scripture itself as it unmasks the deceptions of the devil, which still hold so many in spiritual captivity, through ignorance. Beginning in Genesis with the Fall and working through the whole sweep of Old Testament history, he shows how over and over again God's people have chosen the devil's lies over God's liberating truth. It is a problem of such dimensions that it could, and did, find its solution only in the incarnation of the Son of God, who is Himself the very definition of divine truth. Through His atoning death and glorious resurrection, He has opened a new and living way to God and bestowed on His repentant and believing people the gift of everlasting life. It is this Biblical theology which can deal comprehensively with deception and this book shows us how.

This is a strongly practical book, which gives real help on real issues. Part of its persuasive power lies in the many allusions and examples from our contemporary culture, which define the issues and expose the falsehoods we all encounter, in easily recognizable terms. Its message deserves to be studied by pastors and congregations alike, to become aware of what the Lord is saying to the churches about these urgent and pressing problems. It is a wake-up call which we all need to hear and heed if we are to stand firm in the present crisis and to persevere in godly faith and obedience as the future unfolds. Centuries ago, John Calvin wrote that we cannot rely on God's promises without obeying His commands. This is a book which faithfully and persuasively presents both and from which there are many crucial lessons to learn. I have benefited from it personally and I am sure that many others will too. I warmly commend it to you. It is indeed a much-needed book.

David Jackman

Eastbourne
January 2021.

1.

Introduction:
The Age of Fake

We live in an age that could be dubbed "the age of fake". Fake news stories have become commonplace over these last few years, notably the claim that they influenced the US presidential election of 2016, as well as the EU referendum in the UK in the same year. The events of that year seem to have triggered a rash of publications dealing with the new phenomenon of "Post-truth" (which Oxford Dictionaries declared to be its 2016 international word of the year), written by established political journalists like Evan Davis, Matthew D'Ancona, and James Ball.[1] Politics for many people is synonymous with deceit anyway, but the present spate of political disinformation seems to have plumbed new depths. The four years of the Trump Presidency in the USA have been marked by constant allegations and counter-allegations of *fake news,* culminating in the allegations of fraudulent voting in the 2020 Presidential election. At the same time, social media is awash with conspiracy theories of every currency — most recently, concerning the Coronavirus pandemic, with some suggesting that a gigantic fraud is being perpetrated on the world.

---

[1]   Evan Davis, *Post-Truth: Why we have reached peak bulls — t and what we can do about it,* Little, Brown, 2017
Matthew D'Ancona, *Post Truth: The new war on truth and how to fight back,* Penguin, 2017
James Ball, *Post-truth: How bulls—t conquered the world,* Biteback, 2017

— 1 —

These examples have brought home the enormous potential of the internet to propagate fakery. The digital revolution has made the manipulation of news stories possible on an industrial scale, and when social media is added to the cocktail, we should not be surprised at the explosion of fakery that has followed: the younger generations have become masters of the art of re-inventing themselves on their *Instagram* and *Facebook* accounts; photo-editing is now such a common practice that perhaps we feel the old adage, *the camera never lies*, could almost be turned on its head — *it always lies!* We can manufacture a fake ID for ourselves very easily, and these have been used for such things as financial fraud, online dating and other nefarious purposes on the "dark web". The most recent warning concerns something called "Deepfake", whereby video-manipulation makes it possible to have public figures appear on a screen saying something that in fact they never did — but how to tell? As a portent of this, Channel 4 broadcast an alternative Christmas message, purporting to be by Her Majesty the Queen, on Christmas Day 2020, using deepfake techniques.

Most of us will have been targeted at some point by scammers. On the radio station I listen to most at the moment, the FCA (Financial Conduct Authority) is putting out an advert warning people of fake financial products — scams aimed at conning us out of our retirement savings and the like; annoyingly, banks and financial institutions are forever changing their security checks to prevent fraud; and even as I write this, I have just had what I am sure is a fake phone call, with an automated voice claiming to represent my ISP (internet service provider), telling me I would be cut off from today unless I pressed '1' on the keypad — just one of the many fake cold calls I regularly receive.[2]

---

[2]   Two slightly amusing anecdotes show that even those at the highest levels in government can be taken in by fakery: in this country it was reported in May 2018 that Boris Johnson received a prank call from a Russian claiming to be the newly elected Prime Minister of Armenia, and that a conversation followed in which our then Foreign Secretary discussed UK-Russian relations (in the wake of the Salisbury poisoning) and the Russian involvement in the Syrian civil war; a month later it was reported that Donald Trump had also been taken in by a phone call while on Air Force One from a prankster posing as a US Senator. If you feel a dupe at times, you're in good — well, elevated — company!

1. Introduction: The Age of Fake

On terrestrial TV, *Fake Britain* is a current BBC 1 series looking at all sorts of dodgy dealers trying various other methods to con us out of our money; *Fake or Fortune* is another BBC series given prime TV time, investigating whether artworks are authentic or not (we may not feel this has much application to many of us — though perhaps a similar series could be devised to investigate so-called reality TV shows, which are surely more fake than reality?)

If, like me, you watched much of the 2018 football World Cup, you'll have seen footballers writhing in great agony on the pitch from a supposed foul, only to get up moments later and resume running around normally — the "injury" was entirely fake! Video technology was also brought in for the 2018 competition, partly because fake "dives" are now so common among players trying to win a penalty. And then of course there are the drugs cheats in sport — those from all disciplines whose achievements are not really theirs at all, but belong more to skilled practitioners in the pharmaceutical industry.

Increasing numbers of us are choosing fake grass for our gardens, while fake flowers appear in our homes; fake weddings are used to circumvent immigration procedures; while our very appearances are now subject to fakery — fake sun tans, hair dyes, and various cosmetic treatments and surgery — often to disguise the grim reality of our aging bodies; or more recently to assume a different gender identity.

Of course, fakery is nothing new in this world — it just seems at the moment we are undergoing a rather intense experience of it in all sorts of walks of life. So how can we make sense of this trend? What's causing it? And how should we react to it?

From the Christian point of view, the secular world has only limited answers to these questions. It may indeed recognize the phenomenon, and try to find solutions. The BBC, for instance, recently launched what it called "a huge initiative" called *"Beyond fake news"*, a season of programs and features seeking to identify, understand and then combat this phenomenon. Likewise the journalists mentioned in the opening paragraph all propose methods of halting what one of them calls "truth decay".

By contrast, Christians understand that deception at its heart is a spiritual phenomenon, which secular society struggles to understand. When Jesus spoke to the Jews about truth and falsehood, He labelled the devil as "the father of lies" (John 8:44) — here, He says, is the source of deception: a malevolent spiritual creature whose influence is now reflected in the entire human race. On the other hand, the God presented to us in Scripture is one who is incapable of deceit:

God is not human, that he should lie. (Numbers 23:19)

The words of the Lord are flawless, like silver purified in a crucible, like gold refined seven times. (Psalm 12:6)

God must be absolutely trustworthy in all He has spoken, if He is to be worthy of our reverence; the Bible claims that His very words, recorded by the prophets of the Old Testament, and the apostles (and their associates) in the New, have been *"breathed out"*, as we are told in 2 Tim. 3:16 — that is, they are pristine, reflecting the very character of God. Jesus Himself, in His prayer for the disciples later in John's Gospel, asks His Father to sanctify them by the truth, adding *"Your word is truth."*

The Bible story, in fact — or at least, the major part of it dealing with the human predicament following the Fall — can be seen as "bookended" by the theme of deception: it is at the core of the account of the Fall of Man in Genesis 3 (see chapters 2 & 3 below), and it appears again in Satan's last great roll of the dice in Revelation 20 (see chapter 9 below). It is present throughout the pages of Scripture, which reflect this great conflict between truth and lies, God and Satan; and it is at the heart of the mission of the Messiah, the One sent by God to overthrow the kingdom of darkness that set in after the Fall, and to inaugurate the kingdom of light — the One who declared that He, in Himself, was the Truth. So it is to the Bible that we must now turn if we are to grapple in any way successfully with this powerful phenomenon of fakery that is at work in our lives today.

2.

The Craft of Satan

In Genesis Chapter 3, after the twin account of Creation in the first two chapters, we encounter the character of the serpent. The first aspect of his character that we are told about is his craftiness, and this is clearly in evidence as he beguiles the woman (who is later named Eve). The process by which this happens is instructive, and provides a model of the sort of methods the devil employs.

In fact, the deception has begun even before the serpent speaks! We are told that the serpent was one of the wild animals the Lord God had made and placed in the garden, yet clearly the devil is more than this — he has supernatural powers that go beyond that of a mere wild animal. At the start of the Book of Job, he appears among the angelic hosts who present themselves before God, and it seems most likely that he is some form of fallen angelic being, now inveterately hostile to God. At the end of the Bible, in the Book of Revelation, the devil is identified as *"the great dragon…that ancient serpent called the devil, or Satan, who leads the whole world astray"* (Revelation 12:9).

The appearance of the devil as a serpent (or snake), therefore, seems to be a subterfuge. Even the picture of a dragon, in keeping with the apocalyptic style of Revelation, is most likely intended to be a symbol, in this case of something wholly evil.

This use of subterfuge is a characteristic of Satan that is confirmed in several New Testament instances. The apostle Paul tells us that the devil *masquerades* (2 Corinthians 11:14) — that is, he puts on a mask, and appears as something other than his true self; in this instance, it is as an angel of light. Elsewhere we see him as the instigator of Peter's remonstrating with Christ as the latter spoke about his path to Calvary (Matt. 16:22–23); and in John 13:27 we are told he actually entered into Judas, leading to that disciple's decision to betray Jesus, perhaps the ultimate deception by someone once called a friend. Jesus, knowing what was to happen later, actually refers to Judas as "a devil" (John 6:70). In these examples, Satan was using two of the disciples as cover for his work — in effect, masquerading behind them.

So Satan's deception begins with appearances — when we encounter the devil, he will, it seems, be in some form of disguise. This is something admirably illustrated in C S Lewis's "Screwtape Letters", in a light-hearted and amusing way (Satan hates being mocked!). But at its heart, this is not a laughing matter. I remember my own experience, as quite a young Christian, when I came into contact with a member of the *Children of God* cult that was active in the 1970s. The individual I encountered was, I think, quite a sincere person, but through what he was promoting, I became keenly aware of something quite sinister seeking to lead me astray. I believe the same can be said today of *The Watchtower*, which wields its influence over the Jehovah's Witnesses that you will probably have met on the doorstep. If you have had any prolonged conversation with them, you will have sensed that there is some sort of spiritual power holding these poor people in its grasp — and the same can be said for other cults.

Having begun his deception by disguising his appearance, Satan continues by engaging Eve in conversation.

First, the serpent just throws out a casual question:

"Did God really say, 'You must not eat from any tree in the garden'?"

Now this is not actually a bare-faced lie — but sometimes the closer a statement is to the truth, the harder it is to distinguish the falsehood contained in it. The serpent knows full well what God has said, so why the need to question at all? And what the serpent says is not an accurate portrayal of God's words anyway — he just quotes the negative command (*You must not…*), and applies it wrongly to every tree, rather than just to the tree of the knowledge of good and evil; he makes no reference at all to the positive permission to eat from any of the other trees in the garden. What the serpent has done is what we are warned in Scripture will happen time and time again: God's word will be *distorted* in the first instance, rather than denied outright. When the devil approaches Jesus at His temptation in the wilderness, this is exactly his tactic — he quotes Psalm 91:11–12, referring to God's promise to keep Jesus from harm, but omits the line *to guard you in all your ways* (see Matt. 4:6). God's promises to Jesus were in the context of the Son's obedience to His Father, and not to be taken as a sort of *carte blanche* allowing Jesus to perform dangerous feats, just (in this case) to prove something to the devil that He had no need to prove. Such distortion of God's word is also something that the apostles Peter and Paul warned the early church to beware of (e.g., Acts 20:30; 2 Peter 3:16).

There is something else we should pick up from the serpent's question — its tone. Of course, we can't be certain *exactly* how these words were spoken, but our imagination can surely picture the scene and detect the slight sneer in the serpent's voice in the word *really*. It's that slightly mocking tone I expect we have all used at some point, expressing our disbelief in something or another, and inviting the other person to share our skepticism: *"Did God really say…?"* We will see in the next chapter how this succeeds with Eve, but perhaps for now we can reflect on how often we have heard the same mocking voice speak to us about our faith in the goodness and truthfulness of the living God. *You don't **really** believe everything you read in the Bible — do you?*

The serpent has engaged Eve's attention; he now goes a step further, and tells her, *"You will not surely die"*, directly contradicting what God has said, but cleverly concentrating his attack on just one key point. There is some ambiguity in his words here: does he mean that Eve will never die, or just that this is not certain? And while Eve may be scratching her head to try and work this one out, the serpent delivers his *coup de grace* on the bemused woman, with his interpretation of God's reason for supposedly misleading Eve:

"For God knows that when you eat of it your eyes will be opened, and you will be like God, knowing good and evil."

The implication is that God has a hidden, ulterior motive for keeping her in darkness — it's so He doesn't have to share His position and power with someone else! Actually, Satan is suggesting, God is a selfish, jealous Being who is depriving Eve of what could rightfully be hers — a position of equality with Him, able to determine good and evil for herself, as He does.

This is the knife being ever so stealthily slipped under the rib cage into the vital organs of the body under a cloak of falsehood. The lie is now complete, and at the end it is actually about who God is — His motives, His purposes and His character. God is portrayed as a rather twisted, selfish, deceitful individual. This is the final form deception takes — black is called white, and vice-versa. We find the same state of mind in the teachers of the law in Mark 3:20–30, when they accuse Jesus of having an evil spirit:

"By the prince of demons he is driving out demons," they say.

Jesus's reply is an emphatic denial, followed by a warning that people who have been so completely deceived about His true character are in grave danger of blaspheming against the Holy Spirit — the "unforgivable" sin! This phrase has given rise to much speculation, but here it can simply be understood as the state we reach when we find ourselves in complete agreement with the lie Satan has told us, in spite of the clear evidence from God to the contrary.

This pattern of deception is a repeating one in human history. Consider the following two examples:

In the eighteenth century the European Enlightenment, under the guiding principle of rationalism (which casts doubt on anything supernatural, as it does not accord with the observed laws of nature), asked: *"Did miracles really happen? Is the Bible really an infallible, inerrant book?"*

Building on this, in the nineteenth and twentieth centuries, with the spread of political Marxism throughout large parts of the world, and the triumph of its atheistic philosophy both in these areas and in many of the intellectual bastions of the west, the question became an assertion: *"There is no God; He is dead — or at least, He is redundant, an irrelevance."* (It wasn't just Marxism declaring this, of course — philosophers like Nietzsche were coming to the same conclusion, though through a different route).

In the later twentieth century, and the early years of the twenty-first, the new, militant atheism has moved a stage further: *"God is not merely non-existent, but He* (or, perhaps more accurately, the image of Him created by His antagonists) *is responsible for much of the evil in the world today. The God of the Bible is a warped individual."* The transition to this stage can be seen in the work of someone like Bertrand Russell, and has been followed up in more recent years by Christopher Hitchens, Sam Harris, and others, as we will see below.

A second example can be seen in the popular philosophy of the last half-century or so; it runs as follows:

Stage 1: *"Did God really fix absolute, inflexible moral laws to control our behavior in all circumstances?"* (This was a popular approach in the 1960s, sometimes called *situation ethics*.)

Stage 2: *"We are surely capable of deciding for ourselves what is right and wrong. As long as what we do (especially in private) does* *not harm anybody, it can't be wrong."* (This line of argument was particularly strong in the last decades of the twentieth century when attitudes toward homosexuality were changing rapidly.)

Stage 3: *"If God is opposed to relationships based on monogamous, mutual love, He is a prude, a killjoy, and morally perverse. What sort of a God would deny people the fulfillment of such self-evidently right longings?'* (This approach became prominent during the debate over same-sex marriage in the early years of the twenty-first century.)

Two particular conclusions can be drawn from the above:

i) The first is that Satan's great deceptions appear to be incremental; that is, the final lie is built upon a series of earlier stages which prepare the mind for the denouement. I don't suppose there were many people who in the 1960s would have taken same-sex marriage as a serious possibility — but after 50 years of cultural change, the human mind was prepared to accept this quite readily when it was finally proposed, and it was taken up with great alacrity over the greater part of the western world. We shall return to this subject in the penultimate chapter, when we look at the great deception at the end of human history.

ii) The second conclusion is that the ultimate purpose of Satan's deception is the smearing of God's character.[3] God's great attributes include His holiness, integrity, and righteousness. Light and purity emanate from his very being, and His name — His very nature — demands respect, honor, and worship. This Satan has refused to do, and so the logic of his rebellion demands that he must try all he can to sully God's name, if only to justify his own actions. In fact, the name "Satan" itself, meaning "adversary", points in this direction;

---

[3]   The same objective can be seen in the Book of Job, where Satan's efforts are directed toward causing Job to curse God — to smear his character. Job's great victory — at this stage, at any rate — is that he did not sin by charging God with wrongdoing (Job 1:22; 2:9–10).

while the word "devil", originating from the Greek *"diabolos"*, meaning "slanderer", indicates the means he will use — false speech. He is thus like some demented individual who in his depraved psychological state feels compelled to adopt an adversarial position to God using verbal falsehoods, no matter how perverse; and so we find him trying to project all his own deep character flaws onto his rival. In this, it must be admitted he has had some success in recent times. Take, for example, the interview that Stephen Fry gave on Irish television in 2015, when he described God as *capricious, mean-minded, and stupid … an utter maniac who is totally selfish.* Or Richard Dawkins's assessment of the God of the Old Testament in his book *The God Delusion*, when he described Him as (among other things) *a misogynistic, homophobic, racist, infanticidal, genocidal, filicidal, pestilential, megalomaniacal, sado-masochistic, capriciously malevolent bully.*

It's not hard to see here the same sort of character assassination that the devil pioneered in Eden, and which in our own age is becoming more and more common.

3.

The Folly of Man

Having pointed to Satan as the instigator of deception, it would be easy to blame all that happened in Eden, and in subsequent human history, on him. It would be reassuring to think of ourselves as victims of a vicious con-trick. We would then emerge still as flawed people, granted; but the blame would lie elsewhere — despite our flaws, we would be, essentially, noble creatures trying to do our best in incredibly difficult circumstances … or at least, that is the sort of narrative we would like to believe.

Unfortunately, it's not a narrative that Scripture supports. Satan is the instigator, as we have seen, but we are willing accomplices. We can see this if we go back to Genesis 3 and examine the role of the man and the woman.

The serpent addresses his opening remarks to the woman, and she immediately engages with him in dialogue. There was no need for this — it was the man who had received the command not to eat from the tree, so it should have been him who answered Satan; and in any case, the command was clear and final and required no elaboration. But the woman decides to parley with Satan, to put him right using her own interpretation of what God had said — and she gets it wrong!

"We may eat fruit from the trees in the garden, but God did say, 'You must not eat fruit from the tree that is in the middle of the garden, and you must not touch it, or you will die.'"

In the first place, she minimizes God's bounty. Whereas God had given permission to eat from any tree other than the tree of the knowledge of good and evil, Eve reduces this to just "trees" in general; and in her response to the devil she puts the emphasis on the prohibition, rather than on God's liberality and generosity — already she is focusing on the negative aspect, much to Satan's delight, no doubt!

Even more seriously, she then adds words of her own to what God had said: *and you must not touch it.* Where did those words come from? Not from God, certainly; nor, indeed, from Satan. Actually, they can only have come from her own imagination! Somehow, she has persuaded herself that God said something he did not. All of this may at first sight appear fairly innocuous — after all, none of it actually changes the *substance* of God's prohibition, does it? But, just as with the word *really* earlier, the importance is all in the new tone that these words lend to her reply. There is something written between the lines here, in invisible ink, which Satan reads very quickly. The woman's words carry an undercurrent: there is a hint in them of an over-strict, negative, finger-wagging God — and this Satan seizes upon in his response, as we saw in the previous section, offering Eve an interpretation of God's character which would have seemed to her a plausible explanation of the situation, in her new-found frame of mind.

Through her own folly, Eve's mind has been prepared for the next stage of the fall. We read that she looks at the fruit of the tree of the knowledge of good and evil in a new way; she sees that it is…

❖ good for food — it will satisfy her physical appetite.

❖ pleasing to the eye — it appeals to the aesthetic side of her soul.

❖ desirable for gaining wisdom — it offers scope for intellectual growth.

All of these thoughts are her own — and not one of them pays an ounce of attention to God; she has already become a "practical atheist", ignoring Him in her decision-making and actions, even though she might acknowledge His existence. For his part, although Satan may have set up the original signposts to set her on this track, he has now stepped back, it seems, and is happy to leave Eve to her own devices. So she takes the fruit, eats it, and then gives some to her husband, who also eats — and the awful deed is complete! The man has been strangely absent from the whole drama up until now, but that should not be a plea for mitigation on his behalf. We are told in this verse that he was with his wife at this time, and yet did not say or do anything to prevent it. Although he was the one who had personally received the command from God not to eat this particular fruit, when it came to the crunch (pun not originally intended!) he appears totally spineless; the one who was given headship in the relationship with his wife abdicates the position almost immediately!

So while Satan is certainly the instigator of this whole miserable mess, it is also painfully obvious that the man and woman also bear responsibility for their actions. Quite simply, Satan could not have succeeded without their help. The human heart has been complicit with Satan in this most serious of all crimes — rebellion against God, the Maker of the Universe and Author of all that is good. Such is the folly of Man.

4.

Evidence from the Old Testament

One small step for man … one giant leap for mankind! These words were used by Neil Armstrong when he took his first steps on the Moon's surface. They could equally well, and with greater justification, be used for the Fall. Adam and Eve found themselves banished forever from the Garden of Eden, and from fellowship with God; sin is now the operating principle in their lives, and everything in the new world they have come to inhabit is subject to the law of decay and death — including their own lives; as Paul tells us, *"the wages of sin is death"* (Rom. 6:23). However, from the perspective of this book, there is a further dimension to this new existence, characterized by a third "d": Deception:

They exchanged the truth of God for a lie… (Rom. 1:25)

Adam and Eve had fallen for the lie, and were now to be subject to the curse that followed. In Ephesians, Paul describes the new condition of the human race as

darkened in their understanding and separated from the life of God because of the ignorance that is in them, due to the hardening of their hearts. (Eph. 4:18)

We see this darkness descending like a curtain in the first words Adam utters after he has disobeyed God's command. God calls to him, *"Where are you?"* Adam's response is immediately evasive:

"I heard the sound of you in the garden, and I was afraid, because I was naked, and I hid myself." (Gen. 3:10)

Rather than answer God's question directly, Adam looks for an excuse to explain his behavior — a "blame game" that he and Eve continue to play for the remainder of that chapter. At the start of the next chapter, when God asks Cain the whereabouts of his brother, he strikes a more truculent note:

I don't know; am I my brother's keeper? (Gen. 4:9)

Evasiveness is giving way to something more false and defiant. The disintegration of the relationship continues; at the start of Genesis 6, God speaks of His Spirit

Contending with man, and sees that *every inclination of the thoughts of his heart was only evil all the time.* (Gen. 6:5)

We read that God's heart was so pained by this new state of affairs that He resolved to wipe mankind from the face of the earth through the flood — though in the end, Noah and his family are spared. God's rescue plan for the human race then begins to take shape with the calling of Abraham in Genesis 12. However, it becomes clear very quickly that this has not changed the characteristic of deceitfulness entrenched in the human heart. Consider the following examples from the Old Testament record:

❖ The patriarchs all display a marked tendency to deceive: Abraham is deceived into thinking he can bring about God's promise of an heir by conceiving a son through Hagar — and this on Sarah's advice, a painful echo of what happened in the Garden of Eden. Abraham himself deceives both Pharaoh and Abimelech regarding the status of Sarah, his wife; Isaac commits a similar deception in regard to Rebekah. Jacob's life revolves around deception, first when he acquires the birthright from Esau, then in his dealings with Laban. His very name means *"he grasps the heel"*, or, figuratively, *"he deceives"* — and this is the name which is often used as a synonym for Israel as a people! The sons of Jacob deceive their father in relation to Joseph's disappearance; and even Joseph deceives his brothers for a time when they come to Egypt seeking grain. Their womenfolk are no better: Sarah tells a barefaced lie to the Lord Himself (Gen. 18:15); Rebekah is the one who instigates the deception Jacob practices against his father (Gen. 27:5ff); and Rachel deceives her father in the matter of the household gods she steals, and then conceals, from him (Gen. 31:34–35).

❖ God's calling of Israel out of Egypt was a new beginning for the nation. Among the Ten Commandments, delivered on Mount Sinai, the ninth enjoined them not to bear false witness, but almost immediately, in a manner reminiscent of Adam and Cain (above), Aaron is economical with the truth when Moses confronts him about the golden calf. First, he blames the people for being prone to evil; then he claims,

"they gave me the gold, and I threw it into the fire, and out came this calf!" (Ex. 32:24)

As they continue through the wilderness, Moses sends out twelve spies to explore the Promised Land of Canaan. On their return, ten of the twelve deliberately distort and exaggerate their account (Num. 13:31–33), and the people of Israel are quick to misrepresent the motives of Moses and the Lord in bringing them out of Egypt (e.g., Num. 14:3). According to the Psalmist:

…they would flatter him [God] with their mouths, lying to him with their tongues… (Ps. 78:36)

Then they themselves become victims when they are deceived by the Midianites who are acting on Balaam's advice (Num.

31:16); and after they have crossed the Jordan and entered Canaan, Israel is deceived by the ruse of the Gibeonites, and forced to live with the consequences (Joshua 9).

❖ The book of Judges records Israel in a downward spiral of sin, with deception much in evidence (take, for instance, Samson's casual lies to Delilah when she asks him for the secret of his great strength in Judges 16). Saul, Israel's first king, becomes mentally unstable after his rejection by the Lord, and schemes to take David's life; David finds himself constantly surrounded by lies and deceit among his own people (e.g., Ps 5:9; 41:4–9; 140:1–3), and has to feign insanity himself when he flees from Saul and takes refuge among the Philistines at Gath (1 Sam. 21:13). Most distressingly, he also succumbs to deceit when he commits adultery with Bathsheba, and then attempts to cover up his actions in his dealings with Uriah, Bathsheba's husband (2 Sam. 11:6–17). Shockingly, like Satan, he has become a liar and a murderer (cf John 8:44), and his actions trigger a sad catalogue of deception and turmoil in the royal court, as he finds himself deceived and betrayed by his own sons and servants: Absalom, Joab, Ziba, and Ahithophel. There are points in the narrative when you feel David is at a loss to know whom to believe and trust anymore (see for instance 2 Sam. 19:24–29; 20:4–5).

❖ The history of Israel, as recorded in 1 Kings, is full of examples of deception (see Appendix I — the theme is present from the very first verse). There is an alarming development in chapter 13 when deception enters the ranks of the prophets themselves, those who were specifically commissioned to declare God's truth! Much of this chapter concerns an episode where one prophet lies to another, with fatal consequences. Then Elijah finds himself isolated when he confronts the false prophets of Baal at the court of Ahab and Jezebel; later, when Ahab plots a joint war with Judah against Aram (Syria), the prophets of Israel are summoned for their advice (1 Kings 22:1–28). About 400 prophets agree that the Lord would give Ramoth Gilead into the kings' hands (which is of course a lie); the false prophet Zedekiah is particularly dramatic and impressive, with the iron horns he manufactures, whereas Micaiah, alone, prophesies disaster. Needless to say, he is not believed, although his advice later proves to be correct.

❖ As the kingdom of Judah meets its end at the hand of the Babylonians, lies and deceit seem to reach fever pitch. Jeremiah finds himself repeatedly confronted by false prophets, and even though it becomes clear that God is speaking through him (for instance, when the false prophet Hananiah died, according to Jeremiah's word — Jer. 28:15–17), yet still the people of Israel reject his prophetic ministry; even after the fall of Jerusalem, the remnant who are left in the land denounce Jeremiah as a liar when he counsels them not to return to Egypt (Jer. 43:1–3). The darkness of deceit appears to have enveloped God's very own people, to the point where they are completely incapable of receiving God's truth delivered through his prophet. The remnant of Israel disappears into Egypt, and into oblivion.

Fittingly, it is Jeremiah whose prophecy delivers the most damning diagnosis of the human condition in the Old Testament. He declares,

The heart is deceitful above all things, and beyond cure. Who can understand it? (Jer. 17:9)

When the Bible speaks about the human heart, it is referring to the seat of our human identity, the ambitions and desires that motivate and define us in our lives — and which are now corrupted by sin and deception, so that God is never at their centre, as he should be. Until or unless we receive a new heart, there is no remedy, as Jeremiah says!

The Old Testament examples reveal that our problem is not just that, wittingly or not, we practise deception, such as we saw with Jacob; we are also prone to it — that is, we are easily taken in by lies, and struggle to discern truth from falsehood, as was the case with Israel when confronted by the ruse of the Gibeonites. Worst of all, we fall victim to *self-deception*, as was the case when David committed adultery with Bathsheba. Somehow he seemed to have justified his actions to himself and to be impervious to the truth, until Nathan's parable found a way through his defenses — the sword of God's word proving itself a trusty weapon against the hardness of the human heart.

This capacity to deceive themselves continues and seems to become more prominent as Israel's history moves towards the time of the exile to Babylon. Diagnosing Israel's spiritual sickness, the prophet Isaiah describes the craftsman who fashions an idol from a block of wood:

A deluded heart has led him astray, and he cannot deliver himself or say, "Is there not a lie in my right hand?" (Isaiah 44:20, ESV)

The craftsman, like Israel, is no longer capable of recognizing an obvious lie for what it is. We can see here something of the judgment of God which Paul describes in Romans 1 when he speaks of God handing people over to the fruit of their own sin. The people of Israel have been found guilty, and Isaiah is instructed to deliver this sentence on them:

"Go and tell this people:
'Be ever hearing, but never understanding;
be ever seeing, but never perceiving.'
Make the heart of this people calloused;
make their ears dull
and close their eyes.
Otherwise they might see with their eyes,
hear with their ears,
understand with their hearts,
and turn and be healed." (Isaiah 6:9–10; cf Matt. 13:14–15; John 12:40; Acts 28:26–27)

The darkness that has fallen over their hearts has been confirmed by God's decree; Israel will no longer be able to discern His Word, and therefore cannot receive the healing of salvation that the Word brings. The prognosis seems terminal — yet we still find the same prophet holding out the hope of recovery, and of a new and better kingdom that would remedy all that was sadly amiss in Israel under the old covenant:

The people walking in darkness have seen a great light;
On those living in the land of the shadow of death a light has dawned.
(Isaiah 9:2)

But this would have to wait for the arrival of God's champion, the Messiah, who would dispel the darkness and deceit that both surrounds us, and lies within. Before we consider His coming, we will take a short detour to consider the matter of deception from the perspective of the secular world.

5.

Evidence from the Secular World

God had entrusted the Jews with His very words — but for the Gentiles, the rest of the world's population, it was the natural world which served as a testimony to God, and to what could be known about Him (Rom. 1:18–20). I think it would be legitimate to add also that an impartial survey of human history and culture, even without the aid of Scripture, would offer plenty of evidence to help people with no particular faith background to come to a similar conclusion to that presented in the Old Testament regarding the nature of the human heart, and its capacity to deceive. How often do we hear phrases like:

People are not what they seem; appearances can be deceptive; don't judge a book by its cover; all that glitters is not gold; he/she flatters to deceive?

Such maxims reflect age-old wisdom; it is our collective experience as a human race that people often act deceitfully. I'm sure many of us have been involved in the process of property rental or purchase at some time — was there ever a field of human activity so riddled with half-truths and euphemisms (beginning with the Estate Agent's description of the property)? Perhaps we've had occasion to resort to the legal profession in the course of our lives — would there even be such a profession if we could trust the words of our fellow human beings? Perhaps some of us have been deeply scarred by being betrayed or let down by a close friend or family member, maybe even our spouse, and we form quite strong convictions about how far we will ever trust someone again. Sometimes I read in our local paper about some small kindness done to a person in need, and the latter remarks: *It restored my faith in human nature.* I often wonder what caused the faith to be lost in the first place — and how long the restored faith will last!

One of the most striking recent pieces of evidence of the human propensity to deceive was presented in a *Horizon* program first broadcast on BBC 2 on 29th of August, 2018. *A week without lying* looked at the role deception plays in our lives and in society, and challenged three people (including an Anglican parish priest — of course!) to try and spend a whole week without employing deception in their social and professional relationships. Needless to say, they all failed, to a greater or lesser degree. The program claimed that we each lie on average about nine times a day; that over a week we lie to about one-third of the people in our lives; and that one in five of our social interactions usually involves some kind of deceit.

What was disappointing, however, was the program's ambivalent attitude toward these findings. Deception was viewed as something which is a naturally occurring, deeply ingrained feature of our human nature (maybe a consequence of our evolutionary past?). Rather than being seen negatively, it was accepted as integral to our humanity, and was considered as something which might actually serve society's interests in some ways, as a sort of "social glue"; that is, as long as we all do it, and recognize that it forms part of our social relationships, it can be a useful way of getting along! Just as perhaps we all watch commercial advertising on our screens, knowing full well that what we are seeing is most likely a significant distortion of reality — yet we go out and buy the products nevertheless!

This was a somewhat disheartening conclusion — viewing deception as merely a kind of social convention. Certainly we can all acknowledge there is a degree of social etiquette involved when we are asked, "How are you?" and reply, "Ok, thanks", when in fact we are anything but. However, this is a world away from the vicious, perverted craft practised by people like Josef Goebbels in Nazi Germany, and not to recognize the distinction seems a glaring oversight.

On the other hand, it is perhaps a reaction that is only to be expected from a generation that has been saturated with lies in so many forms over the last few years, especially with the advent of social media and all its capacity to distort, misinform, misrepresent, and manipulate. The recent books by Davis, D'Ancona, and Ball (referred to in chapter 1) also report a sort of tiredness among today's generation with the whole notion of truth: *'Who cares if it's true or not, it resonates with me, and that's what counts as far as I'm concerned!'* How we perceive something has more to do with our sentiments than with objective reality.

For those of us who go back a little further, this current mood has been built upon the chastening experience of the great propaganda lies of the last century — the frenzy of fascist versus communist for much of the first half of that century, and communist versus capitalist in the second half; and more recently the cultural, religious, and political wars around the turn of this century, involving nationalism, ethnicity, racism, feminism, homosexuality, gender identity and Islamism — each with its own spin doctor or apologist; and this is before we arrived at Trumpism and Brexit! Little wonder that many people simply despair of there being anything remotely resembling objective facts, let alone "truth". It might actually be easier just to accept that we are natural-born liars, and go with our gut instincts!

The field of literature offers further evidence of the prevalence of deception in our collective human experience of life. The works of

Shakespeare, our greatest literary genius, are replete with examples. Strikingly, all four of his great tragedies turn on dissimulation and deception — Hamlet, feigning madness at the Danish court; Othello duped by Iago and completely misreading Desdemona's true character; King Lear unable to discern the honesty behind Cordelia's behavior, while naïvely honoring the sycophantic Goneril and Regan; the treacherous Macbeth and his wife, professing loyalty to King Duncan while plotting his murder, and then attempting to lay the blame elsewhere. *All the world's a stage, and all the men and women merely players,* Shakespeare wrote, in *As You Like It*, suggesting that there is something of an act going on in all of us as we live out our lives, as if we are not being quite true to ourselves. The depiction of deception in literature becomes more sinister as history unwinds: at the heart of George Orwell's novel *1984* is the word *newspeak*, denoting a new type of language in which any correspondence to truth has been surgically removed. There are similar presentiments in *Brave New World* by Aldous Huxley, *Darkness at Noon* by Arthur Koestler, and *The Gulag Archipelago* by Aleksandr Solzhenitsyn; these serve as harbingers of the dark world we now live in, devoid of truth.

Of all our modes of artistic expression, though, it is perhaps the TV and film industry that lends itself most naturally to the theme of deception — the tricks and techniques employed by the camera are so clever! How did *Jurassic Park* create such life-like dinosaurs? How did they manage to make *Forrest Gump* shaking hands with John F Kennedy look so realistic? Now those two films came out in the early 1990s, and visual and special effects (especially computer-generated imagery) have moved on enormously since then. When we watch the screen, our eyes are hostage to the film-makers who create their own version of reality for us — or perhaps who just delight to confuse and disorientate our senses, as in films like *The Matrix* and *Inception*.

Our vulnerability to deception was intriguingly depicted in another film from just before the turn of this century, *The Truman Show*. Jim Carrey plays a man who is adopted at birth by a corporation for the sole purpose of filming his entire life for the benefit of TV audiences around the world. Truman has no idea that his life is simply a show, and that for 30 years everybody around him has been living out a deception as part of the act. Eventually he begins to twig that something is wrong … but I won't spoil the ending for any of you who haven't seen it yet! Suffice to say that the film explores this whole matter of living a life that is, in effect, a deception from the very beginning.

TV is perhaps more mundane and everyday, but it too has added another layer to the unreality of our existence. Soap operas have become part of our national life over the last 50 years, purporting to reflect everyday life in some neck of our woods (or, alternatively, "reflecting the latest flights-of-fancy of the script-writers, driven on by the social trends of the day"). Nevertheless, our appetite for these programs seems insatiable. Just before Christmas 2018, the BBC announced that it was going to spend £87 million on a completely new set for its flagship soap, *Eastenders*, to enhance the viewing experience. A completely fake world is being given a facelift at enormous cost in order to keep us suitably entertained by fake characters acting out fake storylines: our willingness to indulge ourselves in such a way at such expense (the cost of the facelift was over one-and-a-half times what was raised by *Children in Need* just a fortnight earlier) must surely stagger us, if we care to think about it. Even this figure is dwarfed by the amount spent on the video-gaming industry, another area of life where we can create our own fantasy world. In America, this figure has been calculated at $36 billion for 2017, and in the UK for the same year it is reckoned at over £5 billion, with both figures set to rise substantially in 2018. I would imagine that during the recent lockdowns in 2020, the figure will have hit new heights.

Sometimes real life itself can seem a little like a soap opera, especially the lives of celebrities, which are lived out under the glare of such intense publicity. Every celebrity has some sort of public profile which will inevitably be at variance with their real life — and how the media love to show the discrepancy between the two when they can! And how shocked we all are to learn that someone who we have thought of as a role model has been living a life that is quite the opposite! But I wonder whether the rest of us are really any different? Or like Hyacinth Bucket (pronounced "Bouquet") in the sitcom, *Keeping up Appearances*, are we engaged in a never-ending battle to keep up an appearance in front of others, while denying what we are really like — especially in God's eyes?

The truth of this has become very painful for many over the last few years, with people in positions of power, trust, and influence finding themselves accused, and often convicted, of some quite serious crimes against those who were either under their power, or duped by the aura of their public persona. Powerful institutions like the BBC, the major banks, the police service, the House of Commons, the major political parties, Oxfam, the Roman Catholic, Anglican and other churches, and some of the most exclusive public schools, have found, sometimes unwittingly, that they have been harboring serious criminal behavior. The government and the monarchy have been embarrassed by the fact that many of the people who have perpetrated these acts have been publicly lauded for their good deeds and invited to Buckingham Palace to receive some of the highest honors our country can bestow! As Isaiah says of Israel:

"For this is a people without discernment." (Isaiah 27:11, ESV)

And as Paul predicted to Timothy,

evildoers and impostors will go from bad to worse, deceiving and being deceived. (2 Tim. 3:13)

One of the major news stories of 2018 in the UK could also serve as a parable of our times. A man and a woman living in the Salisbury area came across a discarded (but not yet empty) bottle of what purported to be branded perfume, and took advantage of what must have seemed a small windfall — only to find that they had exposed themselves to the powerful and deadly nerve agent *Novichok*. How much like Dawn Sturgess and Charlie Rowley are we in the way we so easily accept the lies of our age? For instance, the human narrative about how we came to be on planet earth — that essentially we are simply the product of a freak accident of nature; or our acceptance of the oft-repeated mantra that at heart human nature is "good". Like Eve, as she looked longingly at the forbidden fruit, we end up believing what we want to believe, what our corrupted hearts (or desires) tell us will serve our own selfish interests. And like Eve — and Dawn Sturgess and Charlie Rowley — we are taking in things that will destroy us.

But the secular world does have something more to say than just to confirm our innate deceitfulness. Many philosophers, writers, and poets have explored this moral falseness or emptiness at the heart of our human experience and sought something deeper and more substantial to satisfy our need. Plato was among the first to express this in his philosophy, describing this world as a sort of shadow of a perfect reality existing in another dimension.

This sense of the unreality of this world, and an inner yearning for a more perfect alternative, ruled by a God of truth and love, was expressed powerfully by the American poet T. S. Eliot. It pervades the whole of his landmark poem *The Waste Land,* where London becomes the *unreal city,* and human life appears disconnected from any life-source. The theme continues in his later poem *The Hollow Men*, where he wrote chillingly of the apparent vacuousness of the human soul (both poems written before his conversion). After his conversion, Eliot's poetry took on a more obviously Christian character, but the earlier themes continued. His 1927 poem, *The Journey of the Magi,* includes these words at its close:

We returned to our places, these Kingdoms,
But no longer at ease here, in the old dispensation,
With an alien people clutching their gods.

Eliot's poetry is highly intellectualized, but if we went to the other end of the spectrum, at the popular level, we see people wearing T-shirts with *"Is this it?"* printed across the front, suggesting in our search for meaning in life, somehow our experiences fall short of what we had hoped for.

The book of Ecclesiastes may be part of the Bible, but it reflects a viewpoint from *"under the sun"*, that is, without the perspective of heaven — something close to a secular position. The author sees that the human heart longs for eternity (Ecclesiastes 3:11), but only experiences the frustration of death and futility (or vanity, as the KJV expresses it). Everything seems so pointless, and human beings act with such callous disregard for each other, the author observes. Although the writer of Ecclesiastes maintained a faith in God, his sentiments are not that far removed from those of the atheist French philosopher Jean-Paul Sartre who declared, *"That God does not exist, I cannot deny, That my whole being cries out for God I cannot forget."*

Perhaps the most enduring expression of this, however, has come from the pen of C S Lewis. In his early adulthood Lewis had adopted atheist convictions. He moved to theism around the age of 30, and shortly after completed the journey to Christian faith. These early years outside the faith enabled him, like Eliot, to understand the secular perspective, and perhaps explain why his most popular books — like *The Lion, the Witch and the Wardrobe* — were written with a general audience in mind (which also explains why it has made the transition to film so successfully in *The Chronicles of Narnia*). Four children stumble accidentally into the mysterious world of Narnia, a place that is at once enchanting and beautiful but also mysterious and threatening. Reading it myself as a youngster, I remember thinking how, when the children return from Narnia, the world they re-enter (our world) seems suddenly quite humdrum, drab, and two-dimensional. Even though we know there is an element of fantasy about Narnia, it does somehow seem to be more real than the world the children return to — in Narnia good and evil are in a fight to the death, and telling lies can have deadly consequences (as Edmund discovers). Even though Lewis did not want the analogy with the Christian gospel pressed too hard, it is surely right for us to see that he is presenting us with a picture of a spiritual world beyond our present one which is somehow much more real than the rather mundane, superficial existence which is often our experience in this one.

This yearning for a more spiritually satisfying world beyond our own recurs in much of Lewis's other work, such as when he describes our sense of beauty in things like music:

"These things … are only the scent of a flower we have not found, the echo of a tune we have not heard, news from a country we have never yet visited." (The Weight of Glory)

And in probably his most popular work on Christian apologetics, *Mere Christianity*, he wrote,

"Most people, if they had really learned to look into their own hearts, would know that they do want, and want acutely, something that cannot be had in this world. There are all sorts of things in this world that offer to give it to you, but they never quite keep their promise … If I find in myself a desire which no experience in this world can satisfy, the most probable explanation is that I was made for another world."

Lewis's writing provides a meeting-point for the secular and Christian worlds, together probing the truth about ourselves and our desire for something beyond what this world offers. From the Christian point of view, I know we are sailing close to a dangerous iceberg here. In the early Christian centuries one of the main heresies, *docetism*, proposed something similar, suggesting the illusory nature of this world — that is, this material world is somehow separate from and inferior to the spiritual realm. (This was often explicit in Greek philosophy, and even today is strongly represented in eastern religions like Hinduism and Buddhism.) This gave rise to various forms of false teaching in the early church, notably the idea that God, being pure Spirit, could not reside in a physical body (i.e., in Jesus), and that therefore Jesus could not properly be called God. However, I do not think what I am discussing here is quite the same thing.

When Jesus spoke of this world, the term he used often meant *'this present age'* (e.g., Luke 16:8; 20:34–35). This is a familiar biblical idea, from both Old and New Testaments. Isaiah and other prophets looked ahead to a new age, which would replace the current, corrupted age, and where God would restore all things. This is the age that Jesus came to usher in, and which He will consummate on His return — when the Son of Man returns and restores all things *"in the age to come"* (Luke 18:30).

Or take the parable of the pearl of great price, which Jesus was using to illustrate the kingdom of God: other pearls were quite "real", but the one the merchant found made them all look worthless by comparison.

Similarly, the age to come, which will be glorious and eternal, makes our own age look decidedly second-rate. Paul the apostle writes that this present age is ephemeral, passing away (1 Cor. 7:31); and the apostle John, having described the operating system of this world (*the cravings of sinful man, the lust of his eyes and the boasting of what he has and does*) then wrote in the next verse that the world and its desires pass away (1 John 2:16–17). That is the nature of this world, in the end — it is destined to disappear, and in that sense it is unreal; it isn't permanent. It is a world overshadowed by the lie — the deception practiced in Eden — and it is the lie we live in today. It awaits liberation from this bondage to deception, to be won for it by the One who alone is capable of removing the curse and bringing in a reign of truth to displace falsehood and error — Jesus Christ, the great Truth-teller and Truth-revealer.

6.

The Overthrow of the Deceiver

It is a cardinal principle of Christian teaching that Jesus's earthly origin was not from this world, as we have understood that term from the previous chapter. He was fully human, born of a virgin called Mary, yet He was not of the same fallen nature as our human forefathers. His Father was God, as He stated on many occasions to the Jews (e.g., John 5:18ff). This has huge implications in relation to the matter of deception. Jesus was not subject to the curse from Genesis 3 in the way that the rest of humanity has been; consequently, He always spoke with total integrity. There was no deceit in His mouth, as Peter reminds us, quoting from Isaiah 53 (1 Peter 2:22); nor was He ever subject to deception, despite Satan's best efforts, as we read in Matthew 4:1–11, where He pointedly refuses to enter into dialogue, unlike Eve in Eden, but replies on each of three occasions,

"It is written…"

demonstrating complete faith in what God had said in His Word. He saw clearly what people were thinking in their hearts, such as when the scribes were inwardly condemning Him for (in their minds) blaspheming (Mark 2:8); He could read Judas's thoughts as He shared the Passover with Him for that last time in the upper room (John 13:21–27).

Jesus therefore walked this earth with a completely different perspective from the rest of humanity: He saw spiritual reality clearly. Whereas there is something of the nature of fakery about this world, and indeed about ourselves, as we have seen in the preceding chapters, Jesus was no fake; in fact, He was the authentic man, the real deal. He could not only say (as He repeatedly did), *"I tell you the truth..."*, He could also say, *"I am...the truth"* (John 8:34; 14:6). Over such a man, unlike the rest of us, Satan has no hold, as Jesus tells the disciples before He goes to His death (John 14:30).

Jesus also spoke about Himself as *the true vine*, implicitly contrasting Himself with Israel, the vine which God planted in the Old Testament (cf Psalm 80:8–13). It is not that Israel was something other than a vine (i.e., a bramble masquerading as a vine), but rather that it didn't, in the end, measure up to the standard of vine that God expected from something which He had planted. Israel, we might say in modern parlance, was not fit for purpose.

And the purpose God had in mind for Israel was indeed a great one. Addressing the Servant of the Lord, who is also referred to as Israel, in Isaiah, God says:

"I, the Lord, have called you in righteousness; I will take hold of your hand. I will keep you and will make you to be a covenant for the people and a light for the Gentiles, to open eyes that are blind, to free captives from prison and to release from the dungeon those who sit in darkness." (Isaiah 42:6–7)

This great theme is reiterated in Isaiah 49:6 and 61:1–2 — the latter verses quoted by Jesus as He begins His Galilean ministry (Luke 4:18–19). *A light for the Gentiles* and *restoration of sight* and *freedom for those in darkness* all speak of one of the great objects of Jesus's mission — to lead us out of deception, out of the shadowlands of this unreal world and into the glorious reality of the kingdom of God, a place where, as Jesus tells us in the Sermon on the Mount, this world's values are inverted, and it is the poor and meek who are blessed, not those who push themselves forward and hog the limelight.

This great mission will involve a mighty struggle with Satan, who Jesus describes as the prince of this world (John 12:31; 14:30; 16:11) — that is, the one presiding over the world that is perishing, as we saw in the previous chapter. He is a prince, not a monarch — this is an important difference, as it means he has no ultimate authority, just a derived one, and as we saw earlier, Jesus is not beholden to him in any way. Nevertheless, as Jesus comes into the world, Satan has several advantages in the battle that lies ahead. One of them is the continuing blindness of the human race, which Satan uses for all it is worth to keep even Jesus's disciples from recognizing who he is, and therefore from responding to him as they ought. Perhaps in no other area does Satan work so hard, or are we so obtuse, or is Jesus so frustrated! After all, as long as Jesus continues to be unrecognized by the human race, so long will Satan's rule over the latter continue!

If we delve back into the Old Testament, we will see that this matter of identifying God's messiah is a constant problem for Israel. When Stephen recounts Israel's history in Acts 7, one of his points is that the nation repeatedly fails to recognize the man God has sent to save them: first Joseph, then Moses, then Jesus — each is rejected by Israel.

When God calls Samuel to anoint a messiah to replace Saul, Samuel is sure he is looking at him when he sees Eliab before him, until God tells him otherwise (1 Samuel 16:6–7). Like many before and after, Samuel is taken in by appearances.

And then we discover that the real Messiah will be not David, but the Son of David — but when David has had 19 sons (which does not include sons by his concubines, according to 1 Chron. 3:1–9), how should Israel know which it will be? If seniority, looks, appetite for the job and political nous counted for anything (as they surely would in a modern context), the successful candidate would have been Absalom, as we see in 2 Samuel 15. After Absalom's death, Adonijah appears to have all the right credentials (see 1 Kings 1:5–6, and the material in Appendix I). Many in Israel were taken in by Adonijah, and acclaimed him as king. There is an interesting detail recorded in the narrative here: we are told that Adonijah proceeded to make various sacrifices as part of the ceremony to make him king, these taking place by *the Serpent's Stone, which is beside En Rogel* (1 Kings 1:9, ESV). We can't always know the precise reason why the writers of Scripture included every detail in their narratives, but I can't help thinking that here we are being pointed back to the original deception of the serpent in the Garden of Eden. It's as if the writer is saying to us, *"Can you see? The devil is trying to mess up God's plan by having the wrong son of David anointed as king! But if you avoid being deceived, you will see Adonijah is a fake!"*

Although it was not obvious if you were just judging by appearance, God had in fact already nominated Solomon as king (see 1 Kings 1:17, cf 1 Chron. 22:9; 28:5–6). This was certainly known by Nathan the prophet, so Israel had no excuse — they had simply not gone to the right source (God's prophet) for their guidance, and consequently had been taken in by a false messiah — a story to be repeated many times over, and which is still happening today!

The same pattern can be seen in the Gospels: all of them are concerned, to a greater or lesser degree, with the problem of how the people of Israel, and even the disciples themselves, will be able to recognize Jesus as the true Messiah, the genuine Son of David. *Who is this?* the disciples ask in Mark 4:41, as Jesus calms the storm; *Who do people say that I am?* asks Jesus at Caesarea Philippi (Mark 8:27). When Peter acknowledges that He is the Christ, Jesus reacts as if a miracle has occurred that is greater than anything He Himself has done up to that point — only God could have revealed this to Peter; human insight would never have come to this conclusion! Jesus sees it as a sign that the veil is gradually being lifted, that the disciples are slowly having their spiritual sight restored, even though in the episode that immediately follows, it is clear that Peter's understanding is still extremely limited, as he rebukes Jesus for speaking about His intention to go to His death. In Mark's gospel, this whole episode is preceded with an account of a healing of a blind man — the only occasion when Jesus has to make two attempts to achieve the healing. As Rico Tice points out in *Christianity Explored*, there is a deliberate parallel being made here: performing miracles of physical healing presents no great problem for Jesus; but trying to get human beings, even those who profess loyalty to Him, to see His true nature, is the hardest task He has faced up to this point! I would guess that there are more miracles recorded in the gospels of Jesus healing blindness than of any other infirmity, which I think we can take to be indicative of one of our greatest needs — to be able to see spiritually again.

Later, echoing the lesson of what happened with Adonijah, Jesus warns His disciples,

"See that no one leads you astray. For many will come in my name, saying, 'I am the Christ', and they will lead many astray … if anyone says to you, 'Look, here is the Christ!' or 'There he is!' do not believe it." (Matt. 24:5, 23)

If the disciples had problems discerning the true identity of Jesus, this was as nothing compared to the religious leaders of Judaism — the scribes and Pharisees. From the beginning, there was a willful refusal on their part to consider the evidence of Jesus's claims. Their poisoned minds turned truth on its head and decided that it was He, Jesus, who was the deceiver! So in Mark 3:22, they attribute His miraculous powers to Beelzebub, the prince of demons. Anyone who shows the least sympathy with Jesus (as the temple guards do in John 7:46) is immediately accused of being deceived by him.

Jesus confronts some of them with the shocking reality of their spiritual condition:

You belong to your father, the devil, and you want to carry out your father's desire. (John 8:44)

He tells them that their father is both a murderer and a liar, his two most salient characteristics. And indeed, during the dialogue that follows, the Jews illustrate this perfectly — first they accuse Jesus of being a Samaritan and demon-possessed (the lie), and then they try to stone Him (the murder)!

Their determination to characterize Jesus as the deceiver continues after the crucifixion. Only 24 hours after His death, we read:

"The next day, the one after Preparation Day, the chief priests and the Pharisees went to Pilate. 'Sir,' they said, 'we remember that while he was still alive that deceiver said, 'After three days I will rise again.' So give the order for the tomb to be made secure until the third day. Otherwise, his disciples may come and steal the body and tell the people that he has been raised from the dead. This last deception will be worse than the first.'"(Matt. 27:62–64)

When the resurrection does actually take place, they have already prepared their minds to reject it as a deception! Jesus had earlier spoken of the teachers of the law in Mark 3:20–30, who accused Him of being demon-possessed, as being at risk of committing the blasphemy against the Spirit; here we can see the fruit of this twisted way of thinking, such that these religious leaders are totally incapable of examining the forthcoming historical event with any impartiality. They are totally self-deceived, creating a narrative from their own imagination to satisfy their own appetite for power and influence. Just as at the Fall, Satan seems to have gained complete mastery over their minds.

So, as Jesus goes to the cross, the outcome of the great spiritual battle appears uncertain; the Jewish religious authorities have decisively rejected Him, and despite their protestations acknowledging Him as Messiah, the disciples still flee the scene of Jesus's arrest. Peter even denies knowing Him — another falsehood. Jesus, however, is confident:

"Now is the time for judgment on this world; now the prince of this world will be driven out," (John 12:31)

he says; and in Mark's account of the crucifixion, as Jesus dies, two events are recorded: the temple curtain is torn from top to bottom, and the centurion overseeing the execution declares,

"Surely this man was the Son of God!" (Mark 15:38–39)

The one event marks God opening the way for mankind to enter into His presence again, as the veil of separation is ripped apart — a direct consequence of the sacrificial death of Christ, making atonement for our sin; and the second shows the impact this has on an individual, as the eyes of a Gentile (and a Roman centurion at that!) are opened to see the true nature of the man who has just been crucified as a common criminal.

The curse of sin has been broken! Satan, with all his wiles and cunning, has actually been outsmarted, as Paul tells the Corinthians:

"…we declare God's wisdom, a mystery that has been hidden and that God destined for our glory before time began. None of the rulers of this age understood it, for if they had, they would not have crucified the Lord of glory." (1 Cor. 2:7–8)

In the Book of Revelation, John pictures the overthrow of the prince of this world like this:

The great dragon was hurled down — that ancient serpent called the devil, or Satan, who leads the whole world astray. He was hurled to the earth, and his angels with him. (Rev. 12:9)

Christ has broken the power of Satan to keep the peoples of the world in captivity to deception. Satan's removal from heaven indicates a decisive defeat in this matter, which is illustrated in this passage towards the end of the Book of Revelation:

*And I saw an angel coming down out of heaven, having the key to the
Abyss and holding in his hand a great chain. He seized the dragon, that
ancient serpent, who is the devil, or Satan, and bound him for a thousand
years. He threw him into the Abyss, and locked and sealed it over him,*
to keep him from deceiving the nations any more *until the thousand
years were ended. After that, he must be set free for a short time.* (Rev.
20:1–3; my emphasis)

Some I know will consider the above passage to refer to the
beginning of a millennial age which follows Christ's return.
However, it seems to me to make more sense if we see it as the
great defeat of Satan at the cross, after which the preaching of the
gospel makes it possible for ordinary mortals, like the centurion at
the cross (the nations), to have their spiritual sight restored, and
to be rescued from the kingdom of Satan, where people are held
captive to deceit.

One of the ways to define a Christian is to speak of a person who
walks by faith, not by sight (2 Cor. 5:7). The inhabitants of the
earth (as the Book of Revelation refers to those who are not saved)
continue to walk by sight — that is, they live for this world, for
all it offers by way of power, wealth, sensual indulgence, and so
on. This is what the world sees, and what our human nature lusts
after. Even those with a religious disposition will continue to walk
by sight, unless the significance of Christ's death on the cross is
revealed to them, as we can see in the case of unbelieving Jews in
the time of the New Testament:

*"Even to this day when Moses is read, a veil covers their hearts. But
whenever anyone turns to the Lord, the veil is taken away."* (2 Cor. 3:15–16)

But the gospel is now freely available to all, and by it a Christian
can receive a new nature, a new heart, new desires, and new,
spiritual sight; it is now possible for believers to have eyes fixed on
the eternal, and not on what is temporary and perishing:

"So we fix our eyes not on what is seen, but on what is unseen. For what is seen is temporary, but what is unseen is eternal." (2 Cor. 4:18)

A Christian is someone who has joined the ranks of that great list of heroes of faith in Hebrews 11, who strain their eyes, scanning the horizon for that eternal city that John Bunyan described in *Pilgrim's Progress*, the city with foundations, whose architect and builder is God. Once it was invisible to our eyes, but now by faith in the atoning death of Christ, it has become visible; and daily, as the gospel is preached all over the world among the nations, the minds, eyes, ears and hearts of men and women are being opened to this glorious hope; and Satan, for all his fulminating and fury, is powerless to prevent the spread of this gospel. He knows now his time is short (Rev. 12:12).

7.

Wisdom for the Church from the Holy Spirit

In the film *The Dambusters*, there is a brief moment after Barnes-Wallis's bouncing bomb has hit the target and exploded when we are not quite sure whether the operation has succeeded or not. Then a small crack appears in the dam, water begins to trickle through — and then, suddenly, the entire structure gives way and water floods everywhere. Something similar is happening at the cross: a mighty blow has been delivered against Satan's kingdom, but at first glance, nothing much seems to have changed. The religious leaders no doubt slapped each other on the back, while investing the money that reverted to them following Judas's death on a burial field for foreigners — it was back to the business of running Judaism…

However, the edifice is cracking! The tomb is empty, and the disciples are overjoyed (if still a little bewildered) to meet with the risen Christ. But the real "game-changer" as far as deception is concerned is what happens a few weeks later at Pentecost, when the Spirit is poured out on the gathered disciples, just as the water rushes from a breached dam. In a short time, the number of believers swells from 120 to 3,000, and more are being added daily. As the new church begins to grow and enjoy a rich mutual fellowship, Ananias and Sapphira step forward, attempting to impress the disciples by an act of generosity to match that of Barnabas (see Acts 4:32–5:11). Peter is immediately aware of the deception being perpetrated, and the two deceivers fall down dead when their lie is laid bare before the church.

The event is very significant, even though the actual deception may seem rather paltry compared to some we have seen committed in churches in our own time. However, Luke is here making a deliberate parallel with a similar event in the Old Testament — the sin of Achan in Joshua 7 (see especially vv10–12), where a prominent member of the clan of Judah attempts to deceive both God and Israel by hiding some of the plunder of Jericho in his tent, despite the ban imposed by Joshua.

In both cases, what lies at the heart of the sin is an attempt to deceive God by someone in the ranks of His people (compare Joshua 7:11 with Acts 5:3), which brings down God's wrath in the ultimate sanction of death; in both cases, money or possessions provide the temptation; in both cases, the people of God were about to embark on their great mission — one to build the kingdom of God by conquering Canaan, the other to build it by preaching the gospel to the ends of the earth. The deception appears to be aimed at disabling both enterprises from within, to frustrate God's mission here on earth by corrupting His people on the inside; and in both cases, the deception ultimately fails.

But there are also important differences. Joshua is unaware of the deception practiced by Achan until God reveals it to him, yet Peter is immediately aware of the deception being practiced by Ananias and Sapphira; there is no mention of Satan or the Holy Spirit in Joshua, but Peter tells Ananias that it is Satan who has filled his heart, and that he has not just lied to him (Peter), but to the Holy Spirit; and whereas in Joshua the Israelites experience a serious setback that puts the entire enterprise in jeopardy for a while, Peter's summary dealing with Ananias and Sapphira sees the progress of the church continue almost without a blip!

Now it is true that Peter and the other apostles were gifted with extraordinary powers, as we see throughout the Book of Acts. The gift of discerning spiritual deceit is again in evidence in Peter in Acts 8:18–23 (in the case of Simon the Sorcerer), and Paul showed similar powers in Acts 13:9–10 and 16:16–18 (the cases of Elymas and the Philippian slave girl). We can see the Holy Spirit at work here, acting like a searchlight on the hearts of men and women, able to look into the darkest corners and reveal deceit. The Spirit *"searches all things, even the deep things of God."* (1 Cor. 2:10b)

But even though we may not possess such extraordinary apostolic powers, the lesson of the parallel between Acts 5 and Joshua 7 does seem to point to a degree of victory over deception in New Testament times that was not generally enjoyed by Israel in the Old Testament. Indeed, it is one of the main theses of this book that the age of deception, begun in Genesis, has come to an end, and the gift of the Holy Spirit is the deposit Christians have received which guarantees the dawning of this new age. Wisdom from the Spirit, to counter the schemes of Satan, is the birthright of *every* Christian — not just the apostles.

We can see evidence of this in the way the apostles addressed the churches in their epistles. We have already seen toward the end of the previous chapter how Paul spoke of God's secret wisdom which was destined for the church's glory (1 Cor. 2:6–8). In that same section, he continues:

What we have received is not the spirit of the world, but the Spirit who is from God, so that we may understand what God has freely given us. This is what we speak, not in words taught us by human wisdom but in words taught by the Spirit, explaining spiritual realities with Spirit-taught words. The person without the Spirit does not accept the things that come from the Spirit of God but considers them foolishness, and cannot understand them because they are discerned only through the Spirit. The person with the Spirit makes judgments about all things... (1 Cor. 2:12–15a)

Paul expects the Corinthian Christians — all of them — to be exercising wisdom from the Spirit, and making discerning judgments as a result. When they meet together and speak God's word prophetically (that is, inspired by the Spirit), Paul expects unbelievers to be convicted of their sin, *as the secrets of their hearts are laid bare* (1 Cor. 14:25a). A similar thought lies behind the words in Hebrews, when the writer speaks of the Spirit-inspired word of God penetrating

even to dividing soul and spirit, joints and marrow; it judges the thoughts and attitudes of the heart. Nothing in all creation is hidden from God's sight. Everything is uncovered and laid bare before the eyes of him to whom we must give account. (Heb. 4:12–13)

Like Paul, the apostle James also expects all believers to acquire wisdom from the Spirit. He writes:

*If any of you lacks wisdom, you should ask God, who gives generously to **all** without finding fault, and it will be given to you.* (James 1:5 — my emphasis)

Later in the epistle he defines this wisdom as that which *comes down from heaven* (James 3:17) — that is, the gift of God through the Holy Spirit.

The Holy Spirit is also the *Spirit of truth* (John 14:17), in opposition to the spirit of error, falseness, lying and deception. So, when Paul writes to the Ephesian church, he insists that this power to resist deception, and to live by the truth, should be an absolutely integral part of their new lives in Christ. Consider how often these themes surface in his instructions to them about this new Christian life they are to lead:

"[The pagan lifestyle] is not the way of life you learned when you heard about Christ and were taught in him in accordance with the <u>truth</u> that is in Jesus. You were taught, with regard to your former way of life, to put off your old self, which is being corrupted by its <u>deceitful desires</u>; to be made new in the attitude of your minds; and to put on the new self, created to be like God in <u>true</u> righteousness and holiness.

Therefore each of you must put off <u>falsehood</u> and speak <u>truthfully</u> to your neighbour, for we are all members of one body......

Let no one <u>deceive</u> you with empty words, for because of such things God's wrath comes on those who are disobedient. Therefore do not be partners with them.

For you were once darkness, but now you are light in the Lord. Live as children of light (for the fruit of the light consists in all goodness, righteousness and <u>truth</u>) and find out what pleases the Lord." (Eph. 4:17–25; 5:6–9; cf Col. 3:9–10)

And the apostle John, writing towards the end of the apostolic age, speaks to the next generation of Christians about this equipping with the Holy Spirit:

"But you have an anointing from the Holy One, and all of you know the truth. I do not write to you because you do not know the truth, but because you do know it and because no lie comes from the truth...See that what you have heard from the beginning remains in you. If it does, you also will remain in the Son and in the Father...I am writing these things to you about those who are trying to lead you astray. As for you, the anointing you received from him remains in you, and you do not need anyone to teach you. But as his anointing teaches you about all things and as that anointing is real, not counterfeit — just as it has taught you, remain in him." (1 John 2:20–21, 24, 26–27)

The term "anointed" which John uses here is a phrase which refers to the indwelling Holy Spirit. It is this which enables the believers here to know the truth, which (as in the previous passage from Ephesians) will not only enable them to be truthful people, but will help guard them against being deceived themselves. In fact, it is quite striking that the imperative *"Do not be deceived!"* (or words to the same effect) is found in almost every New Testament letter.[4]

Satan is now a "busted flush". Paul writes of him that *"we are not unaware of his schemes"* (2 Cor. 2:11) — he is like a character who has been unmasked and exposed for what he really is. He can now be confidently named as the real enemy operating behind the wickedness that takes place in our world, lurking in the shadows and dark places — but no longer hidden from view for those with spiritual sight. Christians should take him seriously, but not as one whom they need to fear any longer. The sting of death, his ultimate weapon, has been removed; and his power to deceive has likewise been spiked.

So James instructs his Christian readers,

"Resist the devil, and he will flee from you." (James 4:7, cf 1 Peter 5:9)

And in the great summons to spiritual warfare in Ephesians 6:10–18, Paul tells the church to take its stand against the devil's schemes, taking hold of all the spiritual armor now at its disposal. *"After you have done everything,"* he says in effect, *"keep standing! He cannot knock you down!"*

This is the task given to the whole church, as the Holy Spirit equips her to take her stand on the newly-won ground, and as she prepares for the counter-attack that is sure to come from the wounded foe.

---

4   E.g., Rom. 16:17–19; 1 Cor. 3:18; 6:19; 12:2; 2 Cor. 11:1–15; Gal. 1:6–9; 3:1–5; 6:7; Eph. 5:6; Phil. 3:2; Col. 2:8–23; 1 Thess. 5:1–11; 2 Thess. 2:1–3; 1 Tim. 1:3–7; 1 Tim. 2:11–15; 3:1–4:5; 4:1–8; 6:10; Tit. 1:10–11; Heb. 3:13; 13:9; James 1:16, 22, 26; 2 Pet. 2; 3:17; 1 John 2:18–27; 4:1–6; 2 John 7–11; Jude 4, 16; Rev. 2:14–15, 20; 3:17.

8.

The Dragon Enraged

Human history has turned a corner at the cross; Satan's power is now limited, and the nations can come into Christ's light; the writer to the Hebrews recognized the great victory of Christ on the cross when he wrote, quoting Psalm 8, that God had put everything under Christ's feet, subjecting the world to Him; but then He pointedly observes:

Yet at present we do not see everything subject to him. (Heb. 2:8)

Having told us that Christ has become sovereign over all, the writer quickly pours cold water over our expectations by telling us that this great victory will not be immediately apparent to our eyes. It is a spiritual reality seen by the eyes of faith, but it is yet to be translated into the ultimate reality of a new creation. In fact, the Bible tells us that Christ's great victory over Satan through His death and resurrection has raised the stakes for everyone involved, and brought about a greater intensity to spiritual warfare.

It's not unlike the situation when Moses led the Israelites out of Egypt after the Passover, only to find that Pharaoh had hardened his heart once more and was in pursuit of the fleeing Israelites with a mighty army, determined now not merely to return them to slavery, but to destroy them! The Book of Revelation describes Satan's reaction to his defeat in a similar way:

"Then the dragon was enraged at the woman and went off to wage war against the rest of her offspring — those who keep God's commands and hold fast their testimony about Jesus." (Rev. 12:17) [The figure of the dragon here represents the devil, while the woman represents the true people of God.]

The point of this is that while Satan has indeed been bound, like the strong man in Mark 3:27 (and the picture in Rev. 20:3, referred to earlier), and his ultimate defeat is now certain, he is nevertheless filled with fury, determined to wreak as much havoc as possible in the time remaining to him. Picture maybe a wild dog that has been running out of control suddenly finding itself on a leash — though its movement may now be restricted, it will growl, snarl, bark, and strain against the leash, making it appear in some ways more ferocious than before! This is similar to the image portrayed by Peter when he describes the devil prowling around like a roaring lion looking for someone to devour — yet he can be resisted. (1 Peter 5:8–9)

So it would be a great mistake to draw the conclusion from chapter 6 that the church, or Christians in general, are somehow immune from Satan's deceptions. At his farewell to the Ephesian elders, Paul warned them of the savage wolves he foresaw coming among them, even from among their own number, and he says that night and day he never stopped warning each of them with tears (Acts 20:29–31). The tears seem to indicate that Paul realized that Satan's schemes would enjoy some success — and yet he pressed upon them daily the responsibility of being ready to repel these attacks.

We might wonder at times, in fact, whether the New Testament church was any different from the people of God in the Old Testament — or indeed whether the church today is! But though the New Testament letters sometimes reveal some pretty serious situations in the churches, we should remember also that the very fact they had these apostolic letters, written mostly as correctives to erring congregations, and containing the whole counsel of God (as Paul puts it in his address to the Ephesian elders — Acts 20:27), demonstrates that the solution to deception was in their very hands — at least, for any church that took apostolic authority to heart. The same apostles who had demonstrated supernatural spiritual discernment against Satan, and foiled his schemes, had also given to the churches the necessary wisdom in the word of God to continue the same struggle — and to do so successfully!

So let's consider, then, these stratagems by which the enraged dragon will seek to deceive the church, according to the wisdom of the New Testament writers.

❖ We can be taken in by _appearances_ so easily! Paul wrote to the Corinthians:

"You are judging by appearances." (2 Cor. 10:7)

which, of course, was exactly the mistake Eve made in Genesis 3! In the case of the Corinthian Christians, the rhetorical ability of the super-apostles seems to have impressed them greatly (2 Cor. 11:6), as well as their forceful behavior (2 Cor. 11:20). The Galatians were impressed by those advocating outward circumcision as a visible means of grace; in both these cases, the advocates may even have appeared "sincere", but we must remember that sincerity is no guarantee against error. "Appearance" may also come in the form of reputation, which was the case with the church in Sardis — but Jesus tells us there was no inner reality (Rev. 3:1). And so often we are taken in by what is physically attractive or impressive, as Samuel was by Eliab (1 Sam. 16:6–7), or that which has worldly status (James 2:2–4). Peter counsels Christian women to avoid falling for the lie that real beauty is what is on the outside, but rather to cultivate inner beauty (1 Peter 3:4). The world sets a high premium on outward beauty, but in the end it will come to naught, as with the fate of the beautifully dressed woman in Revelation 17 — in reality, she is the scarlet whore of Babylon, the Mother of Prostitutes, riding on the back of the beast, doomed to destruction.

❖ There are warnings in many places of the deceitfulness of
  riches and wealth. We have already seen this in the example of
  Ananias and Sapphira (Acts 5:1–2). Jesus speaks about how the
  deceitfulness of wealth made the seed of the word unfruitful
  in the parable of the sower (Matt. 13:22), and Paul gives
  a stern warning of the harmful effects of the love of money (1
  Tim. 6:10). We can see plenty of evidence for this today in the
  church, where materialism, consumerism and greed dominate
  so many lives, and deaden the spiritual senses of many who call
  themselves Christians. The church at Laodicea, which receives
  the harshest condemnation of the seven churches in Revelation,
  was completely deceived by its wealth into thinking it had no
  needs, despite being *"wretched, pitiful, poor, blind, and naked."*
  Jesus warned His listeners,

> *"Watch out! Be on your guard against all kinds of greed; life does not
> consist in an abundance of possessions."* (Luke 12:15)

In fact, we can probably widen this category to include
worldliness in all its forms. Paul tells Timothy that the erstwhile
disciple Demas has deserted him *"because he loved this world"* (2
Tim. 4:9), and John warns Christians not to love the world or
anything in it (1 John 2:15). Similarly, James in his epistle writes
of Christians involved in fights and quarrels because they are
being greedy and exhibiting a friendship with the world which
means that they are at enmity with God (James 4:1–4).

We are daily bombarded with all sorts of commercial
advertising, claiming that a particular product can enhance our
lives and bring us peace, contentment, satisfaction, fulfilment
and happiness; that it can give us status, attractiveness, and
influence — and are often told that the benefit to us is what
is uppermost in the minds of the thoughtful people who are
so generously allowing us the privilege of purchasing their
wares! We would all like to think we are not taken in by this,
but I doubt whether we realize how much advertising works

on the subliminal level. The prosperity gospel is perhaps the church's unconscious response to this swamping of our minds with consumerism: we begin to see God as existing, like a major international corporation, to service our needs. Think for a moment about the songs and prayers at your own church: how many of them disproportionately focus on our material, physical and metaphysical needs, as opposed to focusing on God? It's not that the first shouldn't be present at all (the Lord's Prayer teaches us to pray *give us this day our daily bread*), but is there a healthy balance with prayers and songs that focus on hallowing God's name, asking for His kingdom to come, and His will to be done?

❖ Greed in fact, Paul tells us, is a form of _idolatry_ (Eph. 5:5). We tend to think of idols as taking some sort of physical shape — this was what Paul probably had in mind when he wrote of the Corinthians in their pre-Christian lives as being *led astray by dumb idols* (1 Cor. 12:2). The trouble is, idols have a habit of creeping in again through the back door! They are those things that substitute for God in our lives, and until our faith is perfected in heaven, our corrupted hearts will always be drawn to them — often in forms we would not expect. The excellent books by Tim Keller (*Counterfeit gods,* Hodder, 2009) and Julian Hardyman *(Idols: God's battle for our hearts*, IVP, 2010) will certainly disabuse us of any notion that idolatry is a thing of the past for the believer. We should also take note of the simple plea with which John ends his first epistle:

"Dear children, keep yourselves from idols." (1 John 5:21)

As with the Corinthians, it could be that our past habits seek a way back into our lives. After the first flush of excitement following our conversion, we will find times when faith in Christ will disappoint us — not that Christ does disappoint at all, but our expectations can be false, and lead us to seek solace in those things that are more tangible. We may glance again at our horoscopes, hoping for a hint of romance to come up in them (even though such predictions are based on the movements of lifeless, speechless lumps of rock and balls of gas that spin around our Universe — dumb idols indeed!); or perhaps we begin to give undue attention to a particular sports team, a new car, our Facebook page, or a celebrity or entertainer; or become unhealthily devoted to our work, our family, or one of the many other "hidden" idols that Keller in particular reveals in his book. One such idol that can be especially deceiving is religious idolatry. This in fact is the main theme in the letter to the Hebrews, who were drifting back to their old Jewish practices — and it's quite possible that we, too, may hanker after some of the traditional, comforting, culturally-acceptable aspects of the Christian religion, such as artifacts (buildings, church furniture), aesthetics (music, atmosphere), rituals (*"religious festivals, a New Moon celebration or a Sabbath day"* — Col. 2:16) or rules (*"Do not handle! Do not taste! Do not touch!"* — Col. 2:21), all of which can quickly become idols, subtly detaching us from a living faith in Christ.

❖ One of the principal means Satan uses to lead the church astray is to infiltrate *false teachers* into the ranks of believers. We should note the large number of warnings in the New Testament concerning this. From quite an early point in His ministry, Jesus had been warning His disciples of what to expect in the future:

"Watch out for false prophets. They come to you in sheep's clothing, but inwardly they are ferocious wolves." (Matt. 7:15)

Later in the same gospel, Jesus warns the disciples against the teaching of the Pharisees and Sadducees (Matt. 16:6). These people occupied positions of power and moral authority within the community of God's people — and likewise we can expect "sheep's clothing" to include positions of power and influence in the visible church; we are not to be taken in by such outward appearances, if what such people teach is at variance with the faith handed down by the apostles (see the Bible study on Galatians 2:1–16 in Appendix II). During His final address to His disciples, Jesus again warns them of the danger of false prophets (Matt. 24:4–5, 11, 23–26).

So we should not be surprised when we find evidence that, from very near the start, the New Testament church found itself infiltrated by false teachers. Paul was astonished at how quickly the Galatian churches accepted a false gospel (Gal. 1:6). He speaks of them being *"bewitched"* (Gal. 3:1), implying some degree of supernatural deceit. We can see something similar at work when Paul censures the Corinthians:

"I am afraid that just as Eve was deceived by the snake's cunning, your minds may somehow be led astray from your sincere and pure devotion to Christ. For if someone comes to you and preaches a Jesus other than the Jesus we preached, or if you receive a different spirit from the Spirit you received, or a different gospel from the one you accepted, you put up with it easily enough." (2 Cor. 11:3–4)

Paul appears at times to be at his wits' end in knowing how to persuade this church of the imminent danger hanging over them — you can catch a sense of this if you read the whole section of 2 Cor. 10–13. Ironically, just as Jesus was accused of being a deceiver in His own lifetime, Paul has to defend himself against the same charge—and this from those who called themselves believers (see 2 Cor. 12:16–18)!

One cannot read the later epistles of the New Testament (say from 1 Timothy to Jude), as well as Revelation, without being acutely aware that many of these churches had been successfully infiltrated by false teachers. For instance, Paul warns Titus:

"For there are many rebellious people, mere talkers and deceivers, especially those of the circumcision group...[who] are ruining whole households by teaching things they ought not to teach..." (Titus 1:10–11)

The letters to the seven churches in Revelation reflect a similar picture, with the church at Thyatira, for instance, being rebuked for tolerating the false prophet "Jezebel" and her teaching.

Sometimes, like the example of Elymas in Acts 13:6–10, these false teachers may operate outside Trinitarian church structures — we can see this paralleled today in cults like the Jehovah's Witnesses and the Mormons. More typically, they will seek to infiltrate existing churches, such as the Judaizers advocating circumcision in Galatians and the super-apostles described by Paul in 2 Cor. 11:1–15. Today, the presenting issues will often be different — such as the whole debate around same-sex relationships and gender identity — but the underlying issue is the same: the subverting of the gospel given through the apostolic teachings. This calls for the church to be rigorous in its selection of leaders, applying guidelines like those found in 1 Timothy and Titus in particular. It also calls for the teaching of doctrine to be a priority in the church's program of ministry. This won't be attractive to many, but without it Christians become much easier prey for the false teachers.

❖ The reference to selection of leaders cannot pass without some comment on the move to regularize the appointment of women as leaders over churches (and in some denominations as bishops, or the equivalent) over the last quarter of a century or so in particular. Paul was keenly aware of the manner by which Satan introduced sin to the human race, as we saw above in 2 Corinthians 11:3 (*I am afraid that just as Eve was deceived by the snake's cunning, your minds may somehow be led astray...*). He also referred back to the deception practiced against Eve in the Garden of Eden in 1 Tim. 2:11–14, where the events of Genesis 3 are the context for the prohibition within the church on women teaching or exercising authority over a man. This prohibition occurs again in 1 Corinthians 14:33–35. This has become one of the most difficult teachings to maintain in the church in the UK, indeed in the West in general, in recent years, and secular society is astonished that anyone should still hold to it, regarding it as sheer prejudice. Now it is entirely possible that prejudice is at work on some occasions when this view is expressed, but for many Christians it is a teaching derived from a coherent, Bible-centered understanding of God's ordering of human relationships; and in this latter case, Biblical logic suggests that if a church abandons this teaching, it is making itself vulnerable again to Satan's scheming, setting out on that path of incremental stages we saw at the start in Eden. There is a proverb that states that those who forget the past are condemned to repeat it; the spiritual equivalent could apply to those in the church who forget what happened at the Fall; and in the light of what the Bible says lies in wait at the end of the age (see next chapter), this is surely something to be avoided, no matter what society may say.

❖ The Bible also speaks about _false believers_ (2 Cor. 11:26; Gal. 2:4), _impostors_ (2 Tim. 3:13), or _those who say they are Jews_ [i.e., true believers] _and are not_ (Rev. 2:9). Such people may not actually take to the pulpit as false teachers, but in all sorts of ways they will undermine the credibility of the gospel (see for instance Jude 4). Judas is of course the supreme example: not only was he a thief (John 12:6), but in the end he was also the betrayer of Christ. In the situation that the church finds itself in today in this country, such people may well be those pressing in church meetings for more accommodation with the world in those matters where the doctrine of the church is at odds with society's increasing secularism. Genuine believers need to be alert to this danger and to exercise discernment when such people enter the church. It is an area fraught with difficulty, because the spirit of our age is so set on tolerance and would be aghast that anyone's profession of faith should be questioned. This calls for the church to pay greater attention to discipling newcomers, and for church discipline to be taken seriously when those who profess Christian faith stray into error.

❖ We can be taken captive through _hollow and deceptive philosophy_ (Col. 2:8); Paul tells us that this depends on human tradition and the basic principles of this world — that is, it is not founded on the truth of God's word. The Greeks and Romans had their Stoic and Epicurean philosophers, among others, who would propagate a world-view based on their own human logic. Later on, the Manichaean philosophy would exercise a strong hold over Augustine, preventing him from coming to faith in Christ for some time in the late fourth century AD. In the twentieth century, philosophical Marxism held a strong grip over many, preventing them from accepting Christ; scientific materialism, though perhaps slightly weakened by the new openness to spirituality in postmodernism, is still a potent philosophy denying the existence of the supernatural; and postmodernism itself will seek to undermine any claim to absolute truth. Another recent and very aggressive philosophy is that of radical feminism, whose world-view is intolerant of anything that smacks of patriarchy, making it very hard for those influenced by it to accept the Fatherhood of God in the Bible, or indeed to accept the Bible's teaching on the complementarity of male and female. And then at the popular level, there is the philosophy of YOLO—"you only live once"promoted in books like Katie Price's autobiography, which has the same title, which focuses our minds on this life, and dismisses the life-to-come entirely. We may think that such philosophies affect non-Christians more than Christians, yet Paul is writing here (in Col. 2:8) to believers. Perhaps we are more vulnerable to these thought-patterns than we think?

❖ Finally, and perhaps most importantly, we need to recognize that all of these stratagems of Satan can only succeed because of *our own deceitful hearts*. Though our hearts are renewed through the Holy Spirit on conversion, yet they are not completely free of the curse: there is still a war going on in them between our sinful nature and the Spirit, as we are told in Galatians 5:17:

"For the sinful nature desires what is contrary to the Spirit, and the Spirit what is contrary to the sinful nature. They are in conflict with each other, so that you do not do what you want."

And the apostle John warned Christians against this enemy within:

"The cravings of sinful man, the lust of his eyes and the boasting of what he has and does." (1 John 2:16)

It is as these desires of the "old" heart, the sinful nature, come into contact with the world, that Satan will try to manipulate them to lead us astray. Our emotions, for instance, may be deeply moved by a powerful film or drama, whose purpose is to evoke in us sympathy for a lifestyle or beliefs which are completely at odds with the Bible's teaching; or we can be deeply affected by a beautiful melody, even though the lyrics are pointing us in an unhelpful direction.

In the culture we live in today, where there is so much stimulation of our natural senses everywhere we turn, the pressure is on to respond with feelings and sentiment rather than sound Biblical reasoning. Sometimes these emotions can be negative, perhaps aroused by some sense of injury or grievance. We might find ourselves identifying with the Psalmist, who confessed:

"When my heart was grieved and my spirit embittered,
I was senseless and ignorant; I was a brute beast before you." (Psalm 73:21–22)

And the passions we have seen stirred up over the last few years in the arena of politics on both sides of the Atlantic certainly bear witness to this.

Now, of course, we do not want to be devoid of emotion and passion in our worship of God (which is how past generations of Christians have sometimes been portrayed), but nor should we want them to be in charge — they make good servants, but bad masters.

Lastly, there is that most deep-seated and basic bias in our hearts towards *pride* — perhaps responding to the intellectual appeal of a new doctrine, or the possibility of wealth, fame or success giving us pre-eminence among our peers. However it comes, Paul warns us that such a person is *"puffed up"* and has *"lost connection with the head [i.e., Christ]"* (Col. 2:18–19). The same root word for "puffed up" occurs in Paul's letter to the Corinthians (1 Cor. 8:1), where likewise church members are in danger of becoming detached from the body of Christ. Paul has already warned the Corinthians about their boasting in their own wisdom earlier in the letter, telling them not to deceive themselves into thinking they are wise by the world's standards (1 Cor. 3:18); and he pleads with them to be more discerning with regard to themselves in discussing their attitude to the Lord's Supper, which it seems is incurring God's judgment (1 Cor. 11:31).

Writing to the Romans, again in the context of the body, Paul instructs them:

"Do not think of yourself more highly than you ought, but rather think of yourself with sober judgment, in accordance with the faith God has distributed to each of you." (Rom. 12:3)

And in a similar vein, he writes to the Galatians:

"If anyone thinks they are something when they are not, they deceive themselves." (Gal. 6:3)

He then goes on to warn them against comparing themselves with each other, something which the Corinthians had also been doing (2 Cor. 10:12) — a sure path to *self-deception.* We see the seriousness of this when Paul urges the Corinthians to

"Examine yourselves to see whether you are in the faith; test yourselves. Do you not realize that Christ Jesus is in you — unless, of course, you fail the test." (2 Cor. 13:5)

What a terrible thing if we should, like the Jews who confronted Jesus, actually find ourselves self-deceived by our own profession of "fake" faith!

So, we have a paradox: on the one hand, the nascent church has been equipped to resist Satan's deceptions, in a way that was not possible before. On the other hand, there is plenty of evidence to suggest that, even during New Testament times, the church was falling prey to deception. We live in that period of time often referred to as *"the now and the not yet"*, when the final triumph of the church is clearly in view, but awaits its fulfilment — and at times this can leave us with a painful sense of the discrepancy between what we should be, and what we actually are. The battle will be ongoing; Satan's power to deceive will remain possibly his most potent weapon, and one that is deployed with terrifying effect at the close of human history, as we will see next.

9.

Deception at the Close of the Age

The Christian faith teaches that history is linear — that is, it is moving from a starting point to a finishing point, under the direction of a sovereign God, who has a plan worked out from before the beginning of time — *to bring all things in heaven and on earth under Christ* (Eph. 1:10). This is why history has purpose, and why Christians see Christ's death and resurrection in history as the axis on which all history turns. As Paul argues, if the resurrection didn't take place, our faith is futile (1 Cor. 15:17). This is in contrast to the secular view, which generally sees history as fairly random (*one damned thing after another*, as some cynic once remarked), and to the view of much eastern religion, which sees history as more cyclical (such as we see in the Hindu teaching on reincarnation). Admittedly, there are times when the line of progression does not seem very straight to us — but that there will be a grand finale is something that the whole of Scripture unequivocally subscribes to.

Even from the first few verses that follow the account of the fall of Adam and Eve, the Old Testament looked forward to a Messiah to rectify the great harm done in Eden by the first humans, as we read of one born of woman who will crush the serpent's head (Gen. 3:15). That great Messianic hope swells and matures as the Old Testament narrative continues, causing some of the later prophets like Isaiah to burst into rapturous verse as they anticipate this event (see, for instance, Isaiah chapters 11, 35 and the second half of 65).

Of course, in this context, the incarnation of Jesus appears at first a rather damp squib; but His teaching made it clear that the great end was still in sight, and that His earthly ministry was actually the necessary prequel to His great Second Coming — for it would determine the "elect", those who would be vindicated with Him on His return:

"Then will appear the sign of the Son of Man in heaven. And then all the peoples of the earth will mourn when they see the Son of Man coming on the clouds, with power and great glory. And he will send his angels with a loud trumpet call, and they will gather his elect from the four winds, from one end of the heavens to the other." (Matt. 24:30–31)

This moment is the climax of all history, captured in the closing chapters of Revelation which echo the earlier visions of Isaiah. This is the moment when the sky recedes like a scroll being rolled up, and every mountain and island is removed from its place (Rev. 6:14); a glorious new creation, unblemished by sin, is about to be unveiled — the "age of gold", as the Christmas carol *"It came upon a midnight clear"*, puts it. This ultimate denouement to human history is not just the great hope and expectation of prophets and saints throughout the Bible, but also, as we glimpsed briefly at the end of chapter 4, the deep yearning of every human heart, when that yearning is properly understood.

Now, while it is true that Jesus tells His disciples that the exact timing of this event will remain a mystery — He will come *like a thief in the night* — nevertheless He also tells them in the same passage in Matthew 24 that the approach of this grand finale should not take the true believer by complete surprise. He delivers this warning to His disciples immediately after telling them of His return:

"Now learn this lesson from the fig-tree: As soon as its twigs get tender and its leaves come, you know that summer is near. Even so, when you see all these things happening, you know that it is near, right at the door." (Matt. 24:32–33)

There are signs, Jesus says in effect, that you should recognize, which will warn you of the approach of the end; and these signs, as we read about them in the Bible, relate to an upsurge of evil that will precede His coming; an upsurge marked more than anything else by the power of deception in human affairs. What happens at the end of time will, in fact, bear a resemblance to what happened at the start — there is a striking symmetry here: the Bible records that human history began with an overpowering lie, the deception of Satan recorded in Genesis 3:1–6; and it also tells us that it will end with an overpowering lie, as we will see from the evidence below (principally from Matthew 24, 2 Thessalonians 2, and the later chapters of Revelation).

In all three synoptic accounts of Jesus's discourse on the end of the age, the first thing He warns against is deception (see Matthew 24, Mark 13 and Luke 21); and He repeats this warning several times in the same discourse (Matt. 24:4, 11, 24, 26). Both Matthew and Mark record these words:

"For false Christs and false prophets will appear and perform great signs and miracles to deceive even the elect—if that were possible." (Matt. 24:24; Mark 13:22)

The elect are those whose eternal salvation has been determined by God, and over whom Satan has no hold — we have the assurance of Christ that, once we belong to Him, no one can snatch us out of His hands (John 10:28–29). But no one else can lay hold of this promise. The deception that will be practiced by Satan at this time will be of such a cunning, powerful type, that human wisdom and discernment, by itself, will be powerless to detect or resist it. The only thing that will be beyond its scope is to deceive true believers out of their salvation, as it were. Just as in the Garden of Eden, but now with eternal repercussions, human beings whose link with God has been severed will be utterly defenseless against the wiles of Satan.

There are several other references to this *"great deception"* in Scripture. One is the description in 2 Thessalonians 2 of the coming of the *"man of lawlessness"* (who is usually equated with the antichrist in John's letters, and the false prophet in Revelation 13:11–18). The Thessalonians had been subjected to some false teaching and were concerned about whether they had missed the Lord's return! Paul writes:

"Don't let anyone deceive you in any way, for that day will not come until the man of lawlessness is revealed, the man doomed to destruction … The coming of the lawless one will be in accordance with the work of Satan displayed in all kinds of counterfeit miracles, signs and wonders, and in every sort of evil that deceives those who are perishing. They perish because they refused to love the truth and so be saved. For this reason God sends them a powerful delusion so that they will believe the lie and so that all will be condemned who have not believed the truth but have delighted in wickedness." (2 Thess. 2:3,9–12)

This passage depicts a humanity that is deeply impressed with the miraculous, and is powerless to discern that the source of these miracles is not God but Satan. In Revelation 13:13–14, there is a parallel picture of a miracle-working Beast; in Revelation 16:12–14, the picture is repeated with some slight variations — this time, three evil spirits are seen coming out of the mouth of the dragon and the false prophet. These are described as demons performing miraculous signs, preparing the rulers of the world for the battle on the great day of God Almighty; the picture is repeated a third time in Revelation 20:7–10, describing the pattern of Satan's deception before Christ's glorious return. Those coming from a premillennial position will see this slightly differently, of course, but if we understand Christ's thousand-year rule as a symbol of the triumph of His gospel over the period of history since His death and resurrection, and if Satan's binding (Rev. 20:2) is the corollary to this (his inability to prevent the spread of the gospel), then we find here another sober warning of how powerful the coming deception will be before the final end comes — nothing like it will have been seen before in all the Christian ages. It will be a deception of unprecedented proportions.

It is a truth which John presses upon us repeatedly as the Book of Revelation comes to its climax. In Revelation 17:2, he describes how the inhabitants of the earth were intoxicated with the wine of her (the great prostitute's, or Babylon's) adulteries. Intoxication is a state where we are no longer in control of our faculties — we can't think straight, we can't control our physical movements, and we are prey to whomever would take advantage of us — which is exactly what happens to mankind at this time of Satan's release.

In the Biblical narrative of history, there are other markers pointing to this final climax in human history. The Book of Daniel prophesies what seems to be an almost parallel event concerning *"the appointed time of the end"* (Dan. 8:19), when *"a master of intrigue* [will] *cause deceit to prosper"* (Dan. 8:23, 25). This appears to have been fulfilled in the reign of Antiochus IV Epiphanes, a Hellenistic king who ruled the Seleucid Empire from 175 BC—164 BC and exerted a capricious and tyrannical rule over Judea and Samaria, at the end of the Old Testament canon.

Another marker is described in the Book of Jeremiah, where we read the following:

"Babylon was a gold cup in the Lord's hand; she made the whole earth drunk. The nations drank her wine; therefore they have gone mad." (Jeremiah 51:7, cf Rev. 17:2 above)

Jeremiah prophesied, and lived through, the destruction of the Israelite monarchy at the hands of Babylon. Now, at the close of his book, he utters a prophecy about Babylon itself: her triumph will be short-lived, as judgment will fall on her also, and on all those nations who have fallen under her spell, or drunk her wine, as the prophet phrases it. This, to Jeremiah and his contemporaries, would have appeared to be the end of history as they knew it — the destruction of Judah as a kingdom, followed by the brief exaltation, and then the demise, of her conqueror — the latter being at the hands, they would have expected, of the prophesied Son of David, or Messiah.

In fact, a messiah did appear, but it was Cyrus, the king of Persia (see Isaiah 45:1) — much to the consternation of the Jews! What was going on? What we can see now, from the vantage point of the New Testament, is that, as with much of the Old Testament, what we are witnessing is a sort of dry run; and, as John picks up the language of Jeremiah in Revelation, we can see the fulfilment of the pattern set in the Old Testament. Babylon in the New Testament represents worldliness in all its many forms, devoid of any acknowledgement of God and deceitful to the core, and it will go the same way as Babylon of old — except that the Messiah who accomplishes this will be Jesus Christ, revealed from heaven.

We may also perceive parallels here with the Garden of Eden. Satan tempted Eve with all that the world could offer, and she succumbed; God's people in the Old Testament, Israel, likewise succumbed to Babylon — overpowered not just militarily, but also spiritually, as they became inwardly more and more corrupt, and deceived by false prophets (see chapter 4 above, on Israel at the time of Jeremiah); and at the end of Revelation we see the same scenario played out, as the inhabitants of the world drink from this cup, and perish. And just as God promised a Redeemer in Genesis (Gen. 3:15), and preserved a remnant at the time of the Babylonian victory over Jerusalem, so also at the end of time, Jesus has promised us that the elect will be kept from the great deception that is coming on the world, as we saw earlier in Matthew 24.

We might wonder what form the great deception (or "the lie", as Paul calls it in 2 Thessalonians 2) will take? Is there a particular deception that will prove all-conquering? Some grand all-embracing lie which will completely fool the human race — all, that is, bar the elect? What we have seen so far suggests that Satan's deception is incremental; this is the pattern of the Genesis lie, and also of those we have witnessed in more recent history, as discussed in chapter 2. We would expect something similar in this case, as history reaches its climax. Certainly, the foundations for this "lie" seem to have been well and truly laid, in that many of the great centers of learning around the world have fallen into the hands, by and large, of academic authorities that explicitly reject Biblical truth. The Christian worldview is seen in these places as incompatible with the pursuit of academic knowledge, and academics who profess faith find their careers jeopardized (see for example the article by Professor John Lennox in *Evangelicals Now*, March 2019, where he recounts how he was told by a Cambridge Nobel Prize winner to give up his faith if he wanted a career in science).

This attitude has filtered down into the public consciousness, so that it is quite common now for people without any particular grounding in an academic subject to blithely assume that "the Bible has been disproved". This conviction is strengthened by popular TV programs (such as the documentaries narrated by David Attenborough, Brian Cox and others), which specifically exclude, or deny, a Biblical worldview. The *Horizon* program mentioned in chapter 5, which dealt with the subject of lying, could not bring itself to consider a spiritual perspective on its subject-matter — instead, everything was explained through social, psychological and neurological analysis. At the school level, a National Curriculum (developed in the UK since the mid-1980s) has also now made it possible for a monolithic understanding of a particular subject to be taught to an entire generation. I recently listened on the radio to the Chief Inspector of OFSTED (the body charged with ensuring that schools in the UK deliver the National Curriculum) explaining why it was important that every pupil in primary education in the country was taught an understanding of same-sex relationships. Similarly, atheist scientists like Richard Dawkins campaign for textbooks that promote evolution in such a way that the very idea of God as Creator is excluded.

Of course, it is not uncommon for governments to exercise this sort of control over education — there are plenty of examples from the totalitarian regimes of the twentieth and twenty-first centuries — so we should not read too much into these developments in the UK on their own. Nevertheless, if they are a part of a growing academic consensus world-wide (which neither fascism nor communism achieved), we should take careful note — and especially if the lie (the proposition) is accompanied by a liar (the person). In the 2 Thessalonians 2 passage, Paul speaks of a "man of lawlessness" appearing:

"He will oppose and exalt himself over everything that is called God or is worshipped, so that he sets himself up in God's temple, proclaiming himself to be God." (2 Thess. 2:4)

Twice in this same passage (verses 3 & 8), Paul speaks of this person as "being revealed", and in verse 9 he refers to "his coming"; both of these are terms usually reserved for Christ's second coming, so it appears this "man of lawlessness" is trying to anticipate, or replicate, the role of Christ, offering himself to the inhabitants of the earth as a divinely instituted saviour. In return, he will expect to be worshipped as such. We see a picture of this in Revelation 13:11–17, which describes an image set up by the second beast (or false prophet) which all people on earth are required to worship. In the time when Revelation was written, it would not have been difficult to recognize the Roman Emperor in this role. The Emperor Domitian (AD 81–96), in particular, restored the practice of the imperial cult — the deification and worship of the Roman imperial family. He also arrogated to himself the office of Censor, which involved supervising Roman morals and conduct.

Such an antichrist has been identified at other times in history. The Reformers were quick to label the Pope as the Antichrist, and a later generation pondered whether Napoleon might be this man. In more recent times, Hitler, Stalin, and Mao have all exercised a tyrannical power that seemed to fit the designated role very well — and indeed, John tells us in his first letter that there will be many antichrists (1 John 2:18), so this should not surprise us, while at the same time making us cautious about pronouncing definitively on the subject. In the age of Artificial Intelligence and genetic engineering, who is to say what sort of monster the human race might manufacture as its champion?

In summary, then, Christians can expect that there will emerge at some point at the end of history something which is both personal and propositional, a liar and a lie. Both will command near-universal support, and will in many ways ape the role of a Messiah, offering to bring some sort of salvation to the human race. I remember looking at the faces of many in the huge crowd when Barack Obama was inaugurated as President of the United States, and seeing expressions of such great wonder, hope and belief vested in this man. More recently, Science has been hailed as our savior for bringing us a vaccine to counter Coronavirus. As our world staggers from one crisis to the next, each appearing to move us one step closer to global catastrophe, who is to doubt that the billions of people around the world will look with adoring eyes to one who offers them a way of escape from what may come to seem like certain doom?

One further point may be slightly troubling us. The passage from 2 Thessalonians tells us that this great deception at the end of time will be confirmed by God sending a powerful delusion on those who perish. Why, we may wonder, does God do this, and apparently support Satan's scheme? It's not an easy question to answer.

Let's begin by noting, however, that this is not the only occasion in Scripture where this sort of thing happens. We read in the early chapters of Exodus that God hardened Pharaoh's heart, so that he continued to oppose Moses and refused his demand to let Israel go. Pharaoh would not believe the evidence God put before him, and, as a consequence, by the end of the plagues God confirms Pharaoh in his refusal to believe these signs — with devastating results in the destruction of the first-born in Egypt. (Paul refers to this in Romans 9:14–18, defending God's sovereign right to have mercy on whom He wants, and to harden whom He wants.) A similar event occurs in 1 Kings 22, when the Lord sends a deceiving spirit into the mouths of the prophets advising King Ahab, leading him to attack Ramoth-Gilead, and to go to his own death.

In each of these cases, God's actions are a response to the sinful, unbelieving response of the people concerned. Pharaoh arrogantly rejected God's demands that came to him via Moses and Aaron, preferring instead to summon his own sorcerers and magicians to his side — in effect, to invoke the occult against God, a very serious sin indeed. We then read that

"Pharaoh's heart became hard and he would not listen to them."
(Exodus 7:13)

Later, we read that Pharaoh hardened his own heart (Exodus 8:15), and only by Exodus 9:12 do we read that the Lord hardened his heart (this was after the sixth plague). Of Ahab we read in 1 Kings 21:25–26:

There never was a man like Ahab, who sold himself to do evil in the eyes of the Lord, urged on by Jezebel his wife. He behaved in the vilest manner by going after idols, like the Amorites the Lord drove out before Israel.

God had been very patient with Ahab, giving him many opportunities to repent, but he had remained defiant and rebellious — so in the end, God gave him over to the lie he wanted to believe, even though it leads to his death. This pattern of God confirming people in the lie they have chosen to believe occurs again in Romans 1:24f, where Paul writes of God "handing over" those who persist in their rebellion to the consequences of their actions, as we saw at the end of chapter 4. Likewise we read in 2 Thessalonians 2 that those who were to perish

"refused to love the truth and so be saved. <u>For this reason</u> God sends them a powerful delusion so that they will believe the lie…" (my emphasis)

We can see, therefore, that God's actions are an appropriate response to a people bent on opposing Him. *For this reason,* Paul tells us, God acts, just as He did with Pharaoh and Ahab. This is part of God's judgment on sin — that if we *won't* believe, we will eventually reach the point where we *can't* believe, as we saw earlier at the end of chapter 4 in God's solemn declaration to Isaiah (Isaiah 6:9–10).

How vital it is that we hear God's word, and respond to it, while we can — for the time will come, as Jesus says, when darkness will descend:

"Walk while you have the light, before darkness overtakes you…"

And in the world of fakery which we are experiencing today, who knows how close to us that darkness may be?

Putting Wisdom to Work

The Book of Revelation has done much to reinforce the popular image of "apocalypse" as something dreadful and terrifying for ordinary mortals. References to beasts, miraculous signs, deception, forced worship, marks on foreheads, and the infamous number 666, have all served to stir and unnerve the human imagination. We shouldn't be too quick to dismiss this sense of dread as just imaginary; the Bible does warn us of an all-pervasive power and all-encompassing lie that will be foisted on the human race, against which, naturally speaking, it will be defenseless. But wisdom, as we have seen in chapter 7, is the antidote to deception, and through the Holy Spirit it has been made available to those who are "in Christ". Believers in Christ are sealed and protected, and do not need to fear what the world fears. But wisdom does not act like a lucky charm — it does need to be put to work in our lives in practical ways. So in this last chapter we will look at some of the ways we can do this.

❖ Not being gullible or naïve

One of the ways the secular world likes to portray Christians is as kindly but rather gullible and naïve people. Unfortunately, the caricature is not without foundation. In the parable of the shrewd manager, Jesus commends the man for his smart thinking, and then seems to rue somewhat its absence among the believing community:

"For the people of this world are more shrewd in dealing with their own kind than are the people of the light." (Luke 16:8)

John instructs Christians very simply. *"Dear friends, do not believe every spirit* [that is, every claim to spiritual authority]*"* (1 John 4:1).

Presumably John had seen them doing exactly the opposite! And sadly also, history is full of examples of Christians who have shown sometimes extraordinary gullibility, often resulting in tragedy. One such example is the so-called Children's Crusade in 1212, where thousands of young people as well as others were duped into heading to the Mediterranean, and then to Palestine, with the aim of persuading the Muslims to peacefully surrender the Holy Land. Most, it seems, died *en route* across Europe, while some (according to tradition) ended up being sold into the slave markets of North Africa. The susceptibility of Christians to submit unquestioningly to charismatic leaders with visionary inspiration is a continuing feature of this lack of wisdom. Anabaptists in Germany, anticipating the millennial reign of Christ, rose in revolt between 1633–35 and established a theocracy in the city of Münster, falling under the influence of John of Leyden; it quickly spiralled into all sorts of excesses (including, it seems, polygamy), and ended when it was bloodily suppressed. (In our own time, there is a striking parallel with what happened at Waco, Texas, in 1993 under David Koresh, whose Branch Davidian cult began as an off-shoot from the Seventh Day Adventist Church.) Then there are the Christians who were caught up in the so-called *Toronto Blessing* of the 1990s, claiming unlikely miracles, and demonstrating the presence of the Spirit by imitating animal behavior, or collapsing dramatically at the touch of a dominant leader; more recently, thousands of professing Christians followed the predictions of Harold Camping concerning an imminent rapture, some losing their entire livelihoods in the process.

It is perhaps understandable that when people become Christian believers, a certain degree of cynicism is removed from them, and is replaced by a willingness to believe in "good" again — the passage from 1 Corinthians 13 about love "always hoping, always trusting", springs to mind; critics also cite some of Jesus's teaching from the sermon on the mount (such as *"turning the other cheek"* and *"giving to the one who wants to borrow from you"*) as being somewhat idealistic. But this teaching, whatever its exact interpretation, should never be at the expense of wisdom. A little later in Matthew's gospel, Jesus tells the disciples as they set out on mission:

"Behold, I am sending you out as sheep in the midst of wolves, so be wise as serpents and innocent as doves." (Matt. 10:16, ESV)

Jesus expects His disciples to cultivate real discernment as they head into a hostile environment, while not losing their innocence; the two qualities need not be in opposition to each other. And Jesus Himself is a perfect example, of course, of how a person can be full of compassion and gentleness towards some (as when His heart went out to the widow of Nain in Luke 7:13), while on guard against others (as when He warned against the yeast of the Pharisees and Sadducees in Matthew 16:6).

This last reference highlights one of the key areas where I believe God would have us "wise up". Throughout the Old Testament, the greater threat to God's people was always from within. There was certainly great pressure from without, from the great empires of Egypt, Assyria and Babylon; but the greater danger came from treachery within. When the writer of the Book of Kings examined the reasons for the overthrow of the northern kingdom of Israel by Assyria, he was unequivocal in singling out the people's idolatry and unfaithfulness to the covenant, led by King Jeroboam (2 Kings 17:7–23).

David's experience told a similar story. The Philistines he could cope with, but the psalms are full of his appeals to God to rescue him from deceitful people among the Israelites. The Ziphites, for example, a clan from the tribe of Judah (David's own tribe), were ready at the drop of a hat to hand him over to Saul, who was seeking his life (1 Sam. 23:19–20).

Sometimes it was the king who was culpable: Jehoshaphat, king of Judah, allied himself with king Ahab, the apostate ruler of the northern kingdom of Israel. Jehoshaphat tells Ahab, naïvely:

"I am as you are, and my people as your people; we will join you in the war." (2 Chron. 18:3)

The danger becomes immediately obvious (through the prophecy of Micaiah), but Jehoshaphat perseveres in his course of action, and almost dies as a result. He receives a public rebuke from Jehu the seer on his return to Jerusalem (2 Chron. 19:2), but this doesn't stop him from repeating the same mistake later (2 Chron. 20:35–37). Jehoshaphat thought his main enemies were foreign powers, whereas in fact it was allying with the apostate northern kingdom that caused most damage to Judah.

In contrast, Jesus recognized His enemies were primarily from among the Jews, not the foreign occupying Romans (as when He warned His disciples against the yeast of the Pharisees and Sadducees); and He saw also that His death would come as a result of betrayal from someone within His own inner circle (John 13:11). He would have known the broad outline of this betrayal from quite an early point in His life, as it was clearly prophesied in Psalms 41:9 and 55:12–14.

Later, Paul was to underline this danger in his final address to the Ephesian elders (Acts 20:29–31); and in Revelation, it is the character of the false prophet (that is, someone claiming to speak for God) that Christians should be alert to.

Each church needs to decide for itself on what the implications of this are in their own particular circumstances — for instance,

how to relate to other "Christian" bodies who openly reject key
tenets of the faith — but how good it would be to see Christians
and churches showing real discernment and discrimination in
such matters! And how much moral scandal and spiritual and
psychological damage might have been avoided if those with false
or inadequate professions of faith had not been welcomed into
fellowships with open arms, and given opportunity to prey on
believers like wolves among sheep!

"Dear friends, do not believe every spirit…"

❖ Using our critical faculties

John continues:

*"…but test the spirits to see whether they are from God, because many
false prophets have gone out into the world."* (1 John 4:1)

John points to the need for the Christian to exercise careful judgment
in spiritual matters, contrary to the oft-misquoted mantra about "not
judging", taken from Jesus's sermon on the mount (Matt. 7:1). The
latter is more to do with the fault-finding mentality that can exist in
circles where morality is more important than spirituality, and where
people tend to justify themselves by comparison with others.

In fact, the attitude which refuses to judge anything is just as alien
to the Bible's thinking as the one which is constantly opining about
everything. Paul writes to the Corinthians towards the start of his letter:

"The person with the Spirit makes judgments about all things…" (1 Cor. 2:15)

He then berates them for not judging sin in their midst (1 Cor. 5:1–2,
12); later in the letter he calls on them to exercise judgment in the
matter of the exercise of spiritual gifts (1 Cor. 14:29); and writing to
the Thessalonians he instructs them to *"test everything"*. (1 Thess. 5:21)

So keep your critical faculties with you at all times! Ask searching
questions when some new teaching or practice is introduced into

the church — this is what Kevin DeYoung did when American churches began to make common cause with our culture's obsession with same-sex relationships: *"40 Questions for Christians Now Waving Rainbow Flags"* can be found on *The Gospel Coalition* website (www.thegospelcoalition.org). I think we can follow DeYoung's lead here, but extend it to cover a much wider range of issues where the integrity of the church's faith is at risk. So, let's ask:

+ Is Jesus Christ accurately portrayed in the preaching and teaching we are receiving? Is His identity unmistakably the same one that is reflected in the whole Bible, Old and New Testaments? (The question of Christ's true identity is a major concern of all four gospel writers; as Rico Tice says in his *Christianity Explored* course, "If we don't get His identity right, we'll relate to Him in entirely the wrong way.")

+ Is the gospel of Jesus Christ—His death to atone for our sin, and His resurrection to seal our justification—consistently present in the preaching and teaching we are receiving? Do we ever hear "a different gospel" (cf Gal. 1:6)? How would we know if we did?

+ Is the Bible being taught in our church by pastors and teachers who meet the qualifications of 1 Tim. 3:1–12 and Titus 1:6–9? If women are permitted to preach and teach to the main church congregation, was this decision arrived at after full consideration of 1 Tim. 2:11–14 and 1 Cor. 14:33–35? What Scriptures or arguments were used to overrule these texts?

+ Is the Bible being taught accurately and faithfully, not departing from the faith handed down by the apostles and prophets? Could it be honestly said that, were the church a ship, then Christ would be the captain and the Bible the rudder?

+ Are the Scriptures applied to the congregation, without fear or favor? Is repentance regularly called for?

+ Are individuals encouraged to grow in their understanding of the Bible to the point where they can work through issues in the Bible for themselves, or do they remain dependent on leaders to do their thinking for them?

- What pre-occupations are there that might distract the church from its focus on the gospel? (E.g., views on the modern-day state of Israel; excessive attention paid to music; good works becoming a substitute for gospel witness; a social gospel; "charismatic" spiritual gifts becoming the center of attention; physical healings being sought rather than the miracle of spiritual rebirth.)

- How does the "prosperity gospel" manifest itself in the church? (Remember, Satan is subtle, so it may well not appear in the same garb as the more brash African or American versions.)

- If "prophecies" are being given in times of corporate worship, how are these weighed (cf 1 Cor. 14:29)? Are such prophecies given greater prominence than the public reading of Scripture (cf 1 Tim. 4:13)?

- What are the subliminal messages being taught by the way the church operates? Does music (often referred to as "worship") have pride of place in church meetings? What impact does this have on the Bible message? How strongly do personalities influence what happens at gatherings? Does sentiment rule over Scripture when the church makes major decisions?

- How does the way technology is used in your (or your church's) life increase your susceptibility to deception?

- Do the members of the congregation you belong to love Christian theology more than Christian music, or vice-versa? What are the implications in both scenarios?

- Do the songs and hymns that you sing embrace clear Christian theology, or could they be sung equally heartily by people from the cults or other religions?

- While we need to avoid just a social gospel, can we really say that the gospel we preach is accompanied by actions? Do good works adorn it? Or are we in danger of the hypocrisy James speaks of — claiming to have faith, but without the evidence of good deeds to substantiate this?

- Is the church in the world, but not of it? That is, (i) Does the church actively engage with the world (non-Christians) and seek to draw people to Christ through the gospel? (ii) Does it intentionally resist being swamped by the culture of the world? Is the Bible compromised in any area of church life by the culture of the day?

✤ Growing into maturity

When Paul exhorted the Corinthian church to seek wisdom, he referred to the Christian who exercises wisdom as being "mature" (1 Cor. 2:6). This is the state God expects every believer to be moving towards, but, as in real life, there is no short-cut. We have to grow up in our salvation, just as we have to grow up physically, over time. The apostle Peter tells his readers to *"crave pure spiritual milk* [referring to God's word], *so that by it you may grow up in your salvation"* (1 Peter 2:2).

It is not uncommon today to see pictures on our TV or computer screens of people suffering the effects of famine. At the time of writing, Yemen is the country most frequently featured. We grimace at the sight of emaciated bodies, particularly when it involves young children. If we were able to view the spiritual health of church congregations in the same way, how would we react? The writer to the Hebrews paints such a picture of the Christians he is addressing:

"We have much to say to you about this, but it is hard to make it clear to you because you no longer try to understand. In fact, though by this time you ought to be teachers, you need someone to teach you the elementary truths of God's word all over again. You need milk, not solid food! Anyone who lives on milk, being still an infant, is not acquainted with the teaching about righteousness. But solid food is for the mature, who by constant use have trained themselves to distinguish good from evil." (Heb. 5:11–14)

These Christians seem to be almost starving themselves spiritually, refusing to take in food that will help them to grow. How would you describe your diet, as a Christian? Have you been weaned on to solid food yet? What do you need to do to ensure you are being fed properly, and are not becoming spiritually undernourished?

Paul gives us, in the letter to the Ephesians, the definitive New Testament paradigm on Christian maturity:

"So Christ himself gave the apostles, the prophets, the evangelists, the pastors and teachers, to equip his people for works of service, so that the body of Christ may be built up until we all reach unity in the faith and in the knowledge of the Son of God and become mature, attaining to the whole measure of the fullness of Christ. Then we will no longer be infants, tossed back and forth by the waves, and blown here and there by every wind of teaching and the cunning and craftiness of people in their deceitful scheming. Instead, speaking the truth in love, we will grow to become in every respect the mature body of him who is the head, that is, Christ. From him the whole body, joined and held together by every supporting ligament, grows and builds itself up in love, as each part does its work." (Eph. 4:11–16)

We have already mentioned the central importance of taking in sustenance (God's word) if we are to grow, and that appears again in this passage in the reference to the four-fold ministry of apostles, prophets, evangelists, and pastor-teachers; but the emphasis here falls much more on the image of the church as *the body of Christ*. Our growing maturity as an individual Christian cannot be separated from the body into which we are growing — the local gathering of believers, of which each of us will form an integral part. Only *then*, as part of this greater body, will we be in a position to ride through the storms that Satan will throw up, as he masquerades behind *the cunning and craftiness of people in their deceitful scheming*.

Some of us may have had negative experiences of church, and have perhaps developed a certain cageyness when it comes to being committed to a local gathering of believers; it may be that this reaction is justified to an extent, if the churches concerned have not been ministering God's word properly, or not living it out obediently. In this case, the answer is to find a church that does do these things — but just opting out of church life, or keeping it at arm's length, is not an alternative. The epistles of the New Testament, in which the wisdom of God has come to us through the apostles, were addressed to whole congregations, or pastors and elders of congregations, not to private individuals (with the sole exception of Philemon). That is how their wisdom is to be received — corporately. So, for instance, we see in the above passage from Ephesians that our growth will involve our brothers and sisters *speaking the truth in love* to us (cf Col. 3:16); that means we will need to receive their counsel, allowing them to temper our own, at times, madcap ideas or idiosyncratic interpretations of Scripture! We all need some of our rough edges taken off, however painful that will be — and the fellowship of believers is God's gift to us to allow that to happen.

So make it a priority to keep meeting with each other! At the time of writing, the UK is in lockdown due to Coronavirus, and some are unable to meet as they would usually, in church or in their homes. But we can keep in touch in other ways, using one or more of the many digital resources available to us, or even the old-fashioned phone — for those who are struggling in faith, or are house-bound, these can be a lifeline. Just as *Christian* was helped on his way to the Celestial City in *Pilgrim's Progress* by the fellowship, encouragement, and wisdom of companions like *Faithful* and *Hopeful*, so will we be helped to find our way with the prayerful counsel of good and godly friends. As the writer of Proverbs commented:

"Walk with the wise and become wise, for a companion of fools suffers harm." (Prov. 13:20; cf 1 Cor. 15:33)

✤ Being ready!

In almost the last parable Jesus told in Matthew's account of His life, He returned to the theme of wisdom in speaking about the wise and foolish virgins (Matt. 25:1–13). In the story, the bridegroom (who is a picture of Christ) was a long time coming, and the wedding company all became drowsy and fell asleep; when the groom finally arrives, everyone is caught napping! However, the wise virgins have made provision for this, by having jars of oil at hand to enable their lamps to keep burning, and are ready to go with the groom to the wedding banquet — unlike the foolish virgins, who have to go in search of more oil, and miss their opportunity. When they return, the doors are closed, and it is too late to gain entry.

This theme of "readiness" was one Jesus returned to on several occasions, as, for example, in the following parable He told His disciples in Luke's gospel:

"Stay dressed for action and keep your lamps burning, and be like men who are waiting for their master to come home from the wedding feast, so that they may open the door to him at once when he comes and knocks. Blessed are those servants whom the master finds awake when he comes… If he comes in the second watch, or in the third, and finds them awake, blessed are those servants! But know this, that if the master of the house had known at what hour the thief was coming, he would not have let his house to be broken into. You also must be ready, for the Son of Man is coming at an hour you do not expect." (Luke 12:35–40)

The motif of the thief in the night occurs again in Paul's letter to the Thessalonians:

"…the day of the Lord will come like a thief in the night. While people are saying, 'Peace and safety', destruction will come on them suddenly, as labour pains on a pregnant woman, and they will not escape. But you, brothers and sisters, are not in darkness so that this day should surprise you like a thief. You are all children of the light and children of the day. We do not belong to the night or to the darkness. So, then, let us not be like others, who are asleep, but let us be awake and sober. For those who sleep, sleep at night, and those who get drunk, get drunk at night. But since we belong to the day, let us be sober, putting on faith and love as a breastplate, and the hope of salvation as a helmet." (1 Thess. 5:2–8)

Here is another case where the support and encouragement of fellow believers can be crucial, keeping us on our toes, giving us a nudge if we seem to be nodding off! As we read in Hebrews:

"Encourage one another daily, as long as it is called Today, so that none of you may be hardened by sin's deceitfulness ... And let us consider how we may spur one another on towards love and good deeds. Let us not give up meeting together, as some are in the habit of doing, but let us encourage one another — and all the more as you see the Day approaching." (Heb. 3:13; 10:24–25)

The picture of the approaching dawn appears again in Paul's epistle to the Romans. He writes:

"The hour has already come for you to wake up from your slumber, because our salvation is nearer now than when we first believed. The night is nearly over; the day is almost here. So let us put aside the deeds of darkness and put on the armour of light." (Romans 13:11–12)

On the field of conflict, soldiers are often taught to practice the "stand-to" just before dawn; this was the hour to expect an attack, and peak readiness was required. Paul is telling us here that, for the Christian, this is the spiritual time we have been living in, ever since the coming of the Last Days, marked by the outpouring of the Holy Spirit.

One day, in a flash, that day will dawn: the world will find itself confronted by the searing holiness of the returning Son of God, and those unprepared will perish. As He has promised, Christ will send out His angels to gather His followers, the elect. These will be those who are alert and expectant, fully equipped for the needs of that hour, eagerly waiting for Him; those who have not grown weary and tired from waiting, but who remain ever-awake to His words, obeying them as if they were the very clothes (or armor, or equipment) they were wearing. Our final "wisdom", therefore, will be to keep reminding ourselves of this approaching Day, our great hope, and to live lives that correspond to it. May God give us grace so to do!

Appendix I:

Adapting this material for sermons

(for those called to preach God's word)

The staple diet for many of us in our preaching and teaching programs is the consecutive exposition of a book of the Bible, or part of a book, which we believe gives most scope to God's word to speak for itself. However, a short break to follow a topical series, such as "Deception" (maybe followed by a complementary mid-week Bible study), may add a bit of variety to the teaching program and enable a church to highlight — in proper prophetic manner — some contemporary issue which we need to be especially aware of in our own times. The following schemes are of course merely suggestions — there is ample material for many other permutations.

A one-off sermon:

1 Kings 1: Who is the true King of Israel?

This passage offers a dramatic narrative concerning the succession to the throne of Israel; at its heart is the matter of correctly identifying the true, God-chosen, successor to King David. The narrative could be broken up as follows:

vv1–4: **David's last days** (David appears in an unflattering light — his indecisiveness almost plunges Israel into chaos, vv20, 24, 27;

it is clear Israel needs to look for a successor who will be greater than David — see vv37 & 47.)

vv5–10: **The camp of Adonijah** (Adonijah is the obvious candidate to succeed — he has ambition, charisma, seniority and political astuteness; but we note that *Zoheleth* may mean *"Serpent's stone"* (ESV): a hint that Israel is being deceived.)

vv11–48: **The camp of Solomon** (Solomon is not the obvious candidate — he is from an adulterous relationship, young and inexperienced; his camp is made up of people excluded by Adonijah, often "outsiders", at risk of death if the coup succeeds.)

The triumph of God's purposes (God's word tells us that Solomon was the one God had chosen — see 1 Chron. 22:8–10 and 2 Sam. 12:24–25; Nathan's role as the prophet and interpreter of God's word is crucial at this point in the narrative.)

Interpretation and application: Which king are we following? (We can identify the parallels between Solomon and Christ, and see how easily we too, like Israel, can be deceived into following the wrong claimant. Jesus warned that many would come in His name [Matt. 24:4–5] — not just false claimants, but many false versions of Christ that are preached today; but we can be sure of the true identity of Christ if we are instructed by the prophetic word God has given us.)

A series of three sermons: **"Deception - the craft of Satan"**

A series of three sermons could address the subject of "deception" in Scripture thematically, looking in turn at the three elements in the subtitle of the book: Satan, Man and Christ.

i) **Satan: the father of lies.** (John 8:44)

    This sermon would select from the material used in chapters 1, 2, 6 and 9.

    ❖ Introduction: welcome to the world of fake.

    ❖ The devil's first lie: Genesis 3:1–5.

    ❖ The devil as the prince of this world. (John 12:31)

    ❖ The devil's last lie. (2 Thess. 2:9–10; Rev. 20:7–10)

    ❖ Conclusion: Help! Humanity is out of its depth when pitted against Satan!

    ❖ Application: We need (supernatural) help from outside of ourselves! Heavenly wisdom is on offer. (Rev. 13:18a; 1 Cor. 1:30; James 1:5)

ii) **Man: the foolish accomplice** (Gen. 3:6)

    This sermon would concentrate on the material used in chapters 3, 4, 5 and 6.

    ❖ Introduction: the "selfie"—epitomizing humanity obsessed with itself, rather than looking to God. How did this come about?

    ❖ Human complicity in the Fall. (Gen. 3:6)

    ❖ The deceitful heart (Jer. 17:9, human vulnerability to deception, as we see it in Scripture, in history and in present experience; Jesus's analysis—Mark 7:21–23).

    ❖ Conclusion: Rom. 7:24 (*"What a wretched man I am! Who will rescue me from this body of death?"* Only the death and resurrection of Christ can answer this need.)

❖ Application: Psalm 51:10 (*"Create in me a clean heart, O God"*; the miracle of conversion involves receiving a new heart — do we have this?)

iii) **Jesus: the truth and wisdom of God** (Matt. 4:1–11)

This sermon would focus on how Christ confronted and finally defeated Satan (ch. 6), enabling Christians to resist him (chs. 7 and 9).

❖ Introduction: Matt. 3:17, God the Father announces His Son — the true Servant, walking in the steps of Israel to fulfil Israel's mission.

❖ The temptation (Matt. 4:1–11). Examining each temptation in detail, we can see how Jesus succeeded where both Israel, and Adam and Eve, had failed.

❖ *"It is written."* Underlining how Jesus did not fall back on His own authority, but trusted what is written in Scripture. God's word is the sword of the Spirit. (Eph. 6:17)

❖ Conclusion: Jesus is the real deal; He is the Truth, the One who can dispel the lie. He is both the true Israel and also the second Adam, able to restore us to Eden (whose gates are opened to us again after Jesus's final victory over Satan at the cross!).

❖ Application: a fresh realization of the authority of the word of God — and a willingness to come under its authority! Spiritual warfare is now possible; Satan can be resisted for those "in Christ".

Appendix II:

Adapting this material for Bible studies
(for those responsible for this task)

The number of sessions each of these takes up will depend on the nature and size of the group.

1. The churches in Galatia

Paul has to take a stand when even fellow apostles and church leaders are taken in by deception. In chapter 1, having expressed his astonishment at the Galatians' apostasy (1:6–10), he rehearses his own credentials as an apostle of Jesus Christ (1:11–21). Now read Galatians 2:1–5.

What appears to be *"this matter"* (vv3–4) which is the cause of Paul going to Jerusalem and contending for the faith?

What term does Paul use in verse 4 to describe his opponents, and what does he suggest is their motive?

What is Paul's motive in becoming embroiled in this argument (v5)?

How does Paul describe the leaders of the church in Jerusalem? (See vv2, 6, 9). What do you feel he is suggesting by this language? Does this surprise you at all?

Now read Galatians 2:11–16.

Can you think of any reason why Paul might refer to Peter as Cephas, rather than the more common appellation of Peter which he has used earlier?

What had Cephas done that required Paul to rebuke him publicly (vv11–13)? What was the effect of his actions on others (v13)?

Do you think Cephas was really deceived? What do you think is meant exactly when it says that *"Barnabas was led astray"*? What is the root explanation for their actions?

How would you summarize Paul's criticism of Cephas (vv14–16)? How difficult do you think it was for Paul to do this? Why might he have decided not to do it? Why in the end did he decide he had to?

If you are a leader in a church, what lessons do you learn from this whole episode?

If you are a church member, what lessons are there here for how you should relate to your leaders?

If you were in Paul's situation, would you have done the same thing? Why, or why not? Could a similar situation occur in your church today?

2.   The church at Colosse

The themes of "deception", "wisdom" and "understanding" are at the center of Paul's letter to the Colossians. It would be helpful for the group to read through all four chapters in advance to gain a sense of the overall context, and for the group leader to give some brief introduction to the letter — location of Colossae, date of writing, etc.

Consider Col. 1:9–14.

What is Paul's prayer for the believers at Colossae? What are the roles of *"wisdom"*, *"understanding"* and *"the Spirit"* in this?

What is the relevance of the *"kingdom of light"* and the *"dominion of darkness"* (vv12–13) to this prayer?

Consider Col. 1:28.

Why do you think Paul uses the word *"wisdom"* here? How does it relate to the word *"mature"* in the same sentence?

Read Col. 2:1–5.

What sense do you get of Paul's mental and emotional state concerning the Colossians?

How do *"wisdom"*, *"understanding"* and *"deception"* feature in these verses?

Read Col. 2:6–12.

What danger does Paul foresee for the Colossians (v8a)? How does he characterize this threat in verse 8b?

How does verse 11 help us to understand what Paul might be referring to in verse 8b?

Taking vv6–12 as a whole, what can we say are the marks of a genuine faith?

Read Col. 2:16–23.

What are the things that *"have an appearance of wisdom"* (v23)?

According to Paul, why is such *"wisdom"* not genuine?

Why, then, do you think the Colossian church appears to be submitting to this false *"wisdom"*?

How might such notions of *"wisdom"* appear in church circles today?

Consider Col. 3:16 and 4:2–5.

How are ordinary church members at Colossae encouraged to practice wisdom?

(The group could then use what they have gained from the study as the basis of a time of prayer at the close.)